Conversations About Energy

 The Hoover Institution gratefully acknowledges
THOMAS AND BARBARA STEPHENSON
for their significant support of the
Shultz-Stephenson Task Force on Energy Policy
and this publication.

Conversations About Energy
HOW THE EXPERTS SEE AMERICA'S ENERGY CHOICES

Introduction by
George P. Shultz

Edited by Jeremy Carl and James E. Goodby

HOOVER INSTITUTION

SHULTZ-STEPHENSON TASK FORCE ON
Energy Policy

HOOVER INSTITUTION PRESS
STANFORD UNIVERSITY   STANFORD, CALIFORNIA

www.hoover.org

Hoover Institution Press Publication No. 605

Hoover Institution at Leland Stanford Junior University,
Stanford, California, 94305-6010

First printing 2010
16 15 14 13 12 11 10   7 6 5 4 3 2 1

Manufactured in the United States of America

The paper used in this publication meets the minimum
Requirements of the American National Standard for
Information Sciences—Permanence of Paper for Printed
Library Materials, ANSI/NISO Z39.48-1992. ⊗

Library of Congress Cataloging-in-Publication Data
Conversations about energy : how the experts see America's energy
choices : conference report / introduction by George P. Shultz ;
edited by Jeremy Carl and James E. Goodby.
   p. cm.— (Hoover Institution Press publication ; no. 605)
ISBN 978-0-8179-1305-2 (pbk. : alk. paper)
ISBN 978-0-8179-1306-9 (e-book)
1. Power resources—United States—Congresses.
2. Energy policy—United States—Congresses.   I. Carl, Jeremy.
II. Goodby, James E.   III. Hoover Institution on War, Revolution,
and Peace.
TJ163.25.U6C665   2010
333.790973—dc22   2010040887

CONTENTS

PREFACE

On JANUARY 19–20, 2010, the Hoover Institution's Shultz-Stephenson Task Force on Energy Policy convened a conference for the purpose of discussing several critical energy issues. The issues were selected because the Task Force believed they were especially important, not only in terms of improving the nation's energy stance but also in demonstrating the nation's ability to influence events through sound policies at all levels of government. The topics included:

◇ Distributed energy
◇ Energy efficiency
◇ Internationalizing the nuclear fuel cycle
◇ Synthetic biology: issues and prospects
◇ Putting a price on carbon
◇ Sustained support for research and development
◇ Emerging international energy relationships

In addition to members of the Hoover Energy Task Force, other energy experts, entrepreneurs, scientists, and economists participated in the conference, all sharing the conviction that formulating good energy policy is one of the nation's most important challenges. Throughout, the format was designed to encourage open dialogue with the aim of flushing out ideas and recommendations that might improve the performance of the United States in responding to the energy challenge.

At the time of this writing, both the Senate (Kerry-Lieberman, Lugar-Graham, and proposals by Majority Leader Reid) and House (Waxman-Markey) still have major energy and climate bills pending. It is increasingly uncertain that either house will pass substantive legislation during this Congress. But, it is our hope that some of the recommendations we lay out in this book will have an effect on the future energy and climate policies at the state and national levels.

Following the Introduction by Task Force Chair George P. Shultz, we present a summary of recommendations and a presentation of the highlights of the proceedings. These are summarized in dialogue format, edited and condensed for the sake of brevity and introduced with explanatory material on each subject covered.

INTRODUCTION

George P. Shultz

Chair, Shultz-Stephenson Task Force on Energy Policy

OVER THE PAST FOUR DECADES, the United States has been on an energy roller coaster that has landed us, unnecessarily, in a place that is dangerous to our economy, our national security, and our climate.

In 1959, President Eisenhower, concerned that overdependence on imported oil would be a threat to our national security, imposed a quota of 20 percent of consumption on imports. Today, we import over 60 percent of the oil we use.

And causes for concern have increased. The economic impact of dependence on foreign oil has always been apparent as economic recessions have invariably followed significant oil price increases. President Eisenhower's concern about national security has been greatly heightened in recent times because high prices have funneled large flows of revenue to regimes that do not wish us well.

Now the issue of climate change has been added to our list of concerns. Recognition of the environmental risks created by greenhouse gases has heightened apprehensions about our heavy reliance on oil. And it has brought concerns about the

1

use of coal, which produces much of our electricity, into the policy mix.

Now, starting in 2010, we have another chance to get it right—to construct an energy policy that meets these issues in a comprehensive way.

Along multiple dimensions, the energy industry is almost unfathomably large. Reasonable estimates indicate that demand for energy may well grow by about 35 percent by 2030. Scalability, an important attribute for any new energy development, can apply to something big but also to something small that is readily replicable. Over time, significant change is clearly possible. Energy intensity—energy consumed per dollar of gross domestic product (GDP)—has declined by about 1 percent per year over the past two hundred years, but in response to the oil-price shocks of the 1970s, the rate of decline in energy intensity has nearly tripled.

An effective effort to reduce CO_2 emissions or reduce revenues to oil-producing countries must include the developing world. The challenge is that China, India, and other developing countries see limits on CO_2 emissions as limits on economic growth, and, understandably, they will not accept such limits. Efforts to reduce oil consumption and CO_2 emissions must be cost effective if they are to be adopted in the developing world. Over the long run, technology could have a great impact. Cost-effective technology will naturally be adopted by market forces, without government policy, on a global basis. Research into cost-effective conservation measures and clean energy therefore has the potential for significant payoffs.

Energy is a large and critical component of the economy. Getting energy policy wrong and adopting unnecessarily costly, economically inefficient policies will have a significant negative impact on our standard of living. This means that continued efforts to find and develop new sources of oil and gas are essential. And, insofar as the United States is concerned, efforts should be made to develop our own reserves, consistent with proper environmental standards.

Policy Options

The United States should use policies to set conditions for the market that maximize the possibility of desirable results. The marketplace has long demonstrated its superior ability to sort out low-cost, high-quality providers of energy and other commodities, so policies should be designed to promote the operation of the market and fight against the effectiveness of anticompetitive forces such as OPEC.

At the same time, the marketplace by itself does not take into account important considerations such as the costs of pollution and climate change. These costs should be assessed in such a way that the market recognizes them. The problems of national security that arise from unreliable energy sources are an externality to the market, so ways must be devised to deal with these problems. Also, the market does not usually support basic research because market participants cannot firmly capture the benefits of the research. Commercial development, of course, is another matter. So nonmarket sources of support for basic research are needed, and the subtleties of interaction between research and development should be understood—and fruitful means identified—to ease that transition.

Two of these policy areas, supporting basic research and establishing a price for carbon require more detailed consideration.

Supporting Basic Research on Energy Generously and on a Sustained Basis

An essential attribute when considering energy issues is the ability to think long and to think creatively. We need an energy policy that capitalizes on the traditional American strengths of ingenuity and innovation. Inventive juices, once released, will yield important contributions to solving our energy issues.

Immediate results are desirable wherever possible, but real game-changers will take some time to emerge and develop. They will most likely result from a heavy emphasis on basic scientific research related to energy. Government and private foundations need to take primary responsibility for generous and sustained funding of basic research, which is probably the most important undertaking of any prospective energy policy. Recent efforts by major corporations that have joined together to sponsor basic research demonstrate that they understand its potential. Sustained corporate, foundation, and government support will be an essential source of the game-changing innovations that almost surely lie in our future.

Establishing a Price for Carbon Dioxide Emissions

The production of CO_2 creates a significant risk of man-made global warming, a social cost that is not taken into account naturally by market forces. If this cost is imposed by government on all participants, the playing field will be leveled and the production of CO_2 simultaneously reduced.

Currently under debate are two methods for managing CO_2 emissions: a carbon tax and a carbon cap-and-trade system. These concepts share many of the same advantages but also suffer from many of the same problems. For example, a carbon tax could operate with exemptions for a given industry or company in much the same way that credits are given under a cap-and-trade system of taxation. Methods of granting offsets could be used in either case and have similar risks of fraud and abuse. These methods could be imposed at varying stages, from initial production of the energy source to the point of use. In either case, ease of administration argues for imposition at the upstream end.

Most Task Force members are in favor of the carbon tax alternative on the grounds that it is simple, straightforward, and less subject to fraud and manipulation. Those who support the carbon cap-and-trade system stress that it must be modified in some key respects to prevent abuses and point to the relative ease of its adoption from a political standpoint. Yet this system, recently proposed by President Obama and now embedded in an energy bill passed by the House in June of 2009, has been met with considerable hostility by many members of Congress.

Since either method imposes costs on the U.S. economic system, the desire to remain competitive includes a built-in expectation that other countries will take similar action. The costs of adjustment to either policy will be substantial. To minimize these costs, either system should be phased in through an announced schedule that is periodically revisited. For example, a carbon tax might be introduced at a low price and then be phased in through gradual increases until some agreed-upon maximum is reached. At each step, an assessment of costs and benefits should be made.

In either case, since issues involving the appropriate level of government spending and taxing differ from issues of climate change, the system should be designed to operate on a revenue-neutral basis. Using government revenues from a carbon cap or carbon tax to fund unrelated programs confuses the issue. Therefore, any revenues raised from such a tax should be offset by an equal reduction in other types of federal taxation.

If we can learn from the mistakes of the past that we have made in these and other policy areas, we can build a bridge to a cleaner and more secure energy future.

RECOMMENDATIONS

A NUMBER OF POLICY RECOMMENDATIONS emerged from the discussions at the conference, two of which were particularly critical points of emphasis:

(1) *The need to support basic research on energy generously on a sustained basis*
(2) *The need to establish a price for carbon dioxide emissions*

In addition to these points, a few particularly notable themes emerged that fortunately are in tune with American traditions.

First, a successful U.S. policy will be based on the willingness to try innovative policy approaches, with the understanding that only a few will ultimately prove successful.

Second, a successful energy policy will be one that is flexible and reactive in the face of uncertainty and constantly changing circumstances.

Third, a successful global energy system is likely to rely on many local and regional bottom-up solutions rather than top-down dictates from a single international authority.

And fourth, federal funding can close the gap between the research and development stage (pure science) and full-blown commercial operations that can get commercial funding.

Beyond these key themes, specific recommendations in a number of policy areas are summarized below.

Distributed Energy

◊ Increase research and development on means of enhancing generation of electricity close to where it is to be used.
◊ Rebuild the national grid so that it can be more easily "islanded," utilizing distributed generation possibilities.
◊ Evaluate the potential for feed-in tariffs.
◊ Support a Clean Energy Deployment Administration to bridge the gap between small-scale demonstrations and full-scale commercial plants.

Energy Efficiency

In the United States, improvements in energy efficiency can be made at the state and local level, as the state of California has shown. A national energy efficiency policy should encourage leadership by the private sector and by state and local governments. This effort should be supported at all levels of government by the following actions:

◊ Provide easily accessible information regarding energy pricing and consumption and how to reduce consumption while preserving the benefits that energy conveys;
◊ Package energy-efficient products with other useful and attractive features so that incentives to buy such products are enhanced;
◊ Increase the use of information technology to support efficient use of energy;

◊ Adopt standards at the federal, state, and local levels to enhance energy efficiency, for example, in building codes.

The Nuclear Fuel Cycle

◊ The coupling of the likely expansion of nuclear power globally with the absolutely essential task of trying to rid the world of nuclear weapons suggests that this is the time to act to bring the nuclear fuel cycle under control.
◊ A four-pronged approach to the unresolved problem of how to handle spent fuel should be pursued:
   1. research, in association with international partners, on how to develop reactors that would avoid the necessity of separating plutonium or have the potential for high burn-up of uranium and plutonium;
   2. work to create interim storage facilities for used fuel with the ability to retrieve the fuel at any time;
   3. develop "cradle to the grave" fuel services including fuel leasing and take-back options;
   4. continue to look for locations and methods for permanent disposal of spent fuel.

Synthetic Biology

◊ Although "bottom-up" research and development initiatives are the most likely route to innovation, "top-down" guidance from the federal level also is needed. This should take the form of setting national goals in the synthetic biology field so that funding could be coordinated around those broad goals. Incentives, such as prizes, should be built into the system.

◊ Federal funding for foundational research in synthetic biology is needed if the United States is to take full benefit of the national wealth-generation potential of this field and avoid inadvertent events that could cause environmental and safety problems.

◊ Synthetic biology is inherently an interdisciplinary science and this must be recognized in the approach federal funding agencies adopt in their support for foundational research. Improved coordination among these agencies (Department of Energy, Department of Defense, and National Institutes of Health) is urgently needed. Research and development support is much too piecemeal today.

◊ Several mechanisms have been created at the federal and university levels over the years to ensure the highest standards of safety and security (see discussion in text). The mandates of these mechanisms should be reviewed and updated so that research and development, as well as commercial applications, including containment procedures, can be more effectively monitored, and in a timely way.

◊ Innovation is inherently the result of unfettered scientific enquiry and this must be encouraged, if only so that the United States can maintain its technological edge. At the same time, there is an inescapable element of unpredictability in such work and this needs to be taken into account both in funding and in monitoring activities in this field ("DNA shuffling" is an example of a technique that has potentially dangerous consequences). Research into more effective and lower cost vaccines are desirable, partly as a safeguard against the threat or use of pathogens created by sub-state entities.

◊ A mix of proprietary rights and free, open access to information in the synthetic biology field is the best way to encourage research while creating incentives for entrepreneurs and investors. The dividing line should be drawn between the end products, which should be patented, and the tools used to make them, which should be open to promote further innovation and development.

◊ A dialogue with the public is needed in order to explain more fully and clearly what synthetic biology can offer to the economy and to quality of life. This should avoid "over-branding" and hyperbole and should explain what is being done both to advance the science and to deal with the unintended consequences.

Putting a Price on Carbon

◊ A pure cap-and-trade system is a poor idea, and we should work to avoid this solution in favor of some form of a carbon tax or a cap-and-trade system with a safety valve price. But while cap-and-trade is not the ideal system, even this is preferable to inaction.

◊ The cap should have a price floor as well as a price ceiling in order to avoid artificially skewing prices downward. However, there is a possibility that such ceilings would leave people open to price manipulation, a subject which needs more empirical study.

◊ Offsets in either a cap-and-trade or carbon-tax market need to be looked at with great skepticism. There is a high potential for abuse of a system that is too generous with offsets.

◊ Whatever resources are collected by a cap-and-trade tax or a carbon tax should be refunded to the general public. A revenue-neutral system will then not be a tax drag on the economy.

Sustained Support for Research and Development

A basic component of American national policy must be to establish and maintain a strong research and development program that advances the goal of achieving energy efficiency and independence with technologies that are safe and environmentally friendly. What is needed is: adequate, steady support for a broad scientific and technical base for the program that would encourage both transformative scientific discoveries and directed programmatic advances. And specifically:

⬧ A balanced program based on these principles to attract the top quality scientists and engineers that are critical for success.

⬧ To the greatest degree possible, not to pick technology winners at the Federal Government level.

⬧ For the Federal Government to focus intensively on creating an environment to nurture a broad suite of technologies, paying particular attention to the gap between basic research and projects that are mature enough to receive venture funding.

Emerging International Energy Relationships

⬧ We need to end the phase of hyper-multilateralism in international energy and climate negotiations in favor of bilateral and small-group multilateral engagement.

⬧ Climate negotiations are most likely to be successful in the context of broader energy and trade negotiations, which have greater salience for most countries.

⬧ International energy negotiations should emphasize interdependent commitments, where each country agrees to do a certain set of things, and then to do another set of things if other countries will take on commensurate commitments (World Trade Organization accession talks are a possible model).

◊ It is probably not desirable to create a global carbon price or market—small local and regional markets will do a better job of providing accountability and reasonable pricing.

◊ Investing in technological innovation will be absolutely critical for facilitating more useful negotiations on both climate and energy security because negotiators need to be able to see an economically and politically viable transition path before they will abandon old technologies.

SESSION 1

Distributed Energy

"All of our other seventeen critical infrastructures—so declared by the government because they are essential to basic life, such as water and communications— depend on electricity."

—R. JAMES WOOLSEY

Overview

As THE VULNERABILITY of America's traditional, largely fossil-fuel-powered electricity grid has soared over the past few years, the issue of distributed energy, long a province of esoteric "off grid" devotees, has increasingly moved into the energy mainstream. Distributed energy has many advantages over traditional grid systems—it is potentially more stable and less prone to catastrophe or terrorism.

One example of the failure of a nondistributed grid is the famous Northeastern blackout of 2003, where a few untrimmed trees in a Cleveland, Ohio, suburb caused a local power line failure that eventually cascaded throughout the eastern United States and Canada, affecting 55 million people, leaving them without power for hours.

In addition to its stability advantages, distributed energy also has the potential for being cleaner—many distributed energy systems are small-scale renewables or natural gas, the cleanest fossil fuel.

To discuss the prospects and challenges for distributed energy, the Energy Task Force convened a session led by R. James Woolsey, former director of Central Intelligence, and a longtime leader in the energy policy field, particularly in issues related to energy security. Serving as a discussant was Dan Reicher, the director of Climate and Energy Initiatives at Google.org. Reicher served as assistant secretary of energy for efficiency and renewable energy in the Clinton administration and brings decades of experience in the energy and environmental policy fields to his work at Google.

The conversation focused on applications of distributed energy, the problems of bringing renewables on to the grid, the efficiency of feed-in tariffs, and the security benefits of distributed generation. There was considerable agreement about the positive role that distributed energy can play in boosting renewables, and there was also broad agreement on its positive implications for energy security. There was intense discussion, however, over the issue of feed-in tariffs (policies that essentially obligate utilities to buy power from small-scale renewable energy producers such as farms and businesses with solar and other renewable power installations) and whether it was economically efficient to use this technique to grow renewable energy.

Proceedings

Woolsey began the proceedings by noting that distributed energy is inherently a more secure solution than more traditional forms of electricity delivery and has security implications.

> Distributed generation of energy is defined as a distributed grid that uses energy produced close to where it is consumed and that can "island" to secure itself from cascading grid failure while maintaining electricity to local communities. This should be a key part of solving the complex mix of energy problems we face. When the electrical grid fails, it is not only the lights that go out. All of our other seventeen critical infrastructures—so declared by the government because they are essential to basic life, such as water and communications—depend on electricity. Our grid vulnerability means that our water, sewage, phone, transportation systems, health care, and most of the country's basic economic functions are all easily threatened by both malevolent threats (such as terrorists) and malignant threats (such as tree branches).

Woolsey noted that the key to doing this is to separate the grid into microgrids and minigrids that would prevent a single point of failure.

> The grid should be much more resilient, so it can island into microgrids that protect neighborhoods and minigrids that protect towns in the event of an outage, preventing a single failure from cascading into a catastrophe. But we need not all become survivalists to be somewhat safer. The vast majority of homes and businesses would stay connected to the grid but would harness natural gas as well as solar, wind, geothermal, and other local renewable energy sources for an important share of their power needs.

Woolsey also noted that a better distributed energy grid would allow new economies to develop.

> New policies could force utilities to allow feed-in tariffs, enabling individuals to sell the electricity they generate in excess of their own needs back to the grid and to earn money on their investment. We would still have a national grid, of course. We would simply build into our existing grid the capability to island and separate when need be.

Woolsey added that while such a distributed grid might not be able to have large industrial processes functioning through a major blackout, it would do fine at a household level or at medical facilities, where most pressing needs occurred.

> The microgrid could provide most households, hospitals, schools, and businesses with enough light, refrigeration, and other necessities to function during even a long-term emergency, rather that forcing populations to face the cascading total failure of light, water, heat, and other infrastructure that an attack would cause today. By creating microgrids and minigrids, we could have both the benefits of a national grid system and also the resilience of distributed, independent generating capacity.

Woolsey also discussed what he thought the nature of future developments in renewable energy would look like.

> Rapid expansion of renewables is more likely to come from small- and medium-sized commercial facilities of less than 20 megawatts. To be commercially viable and create a market, utilities would need to allow entrepreneurs who install renewable energy platforms at a small commercial scale to sell their electricity back to the grid.

He argued that existing players in the market are the biggest current obstacles to reform.

Utilities—often mired in their ways, with little incentive to change—have not been advocates of a system that forces them to enable such energy entrepreneurship, and neither have most public utility commissions. But Germany, some forty other countries, Ontario, Hawaii, Vermont, and other localities that have established such feed-in tariffs have discovered—no great surprise—that allowing entrepreneurs to make a profit on the energy they generate creates a market, jobs, and more renewable energy.

Woolsey also said that in the developing world, a centralized grid model, rather than distributed energy, has made the entire electricity system unworkable in many areas.

In much of the developing world, centralized grids never developed. Thus, for over a billion people, electricity remains a distant dream. Big, centralized power plants require significant up-front capital investment—saddling developing countries with debt decades before they begin operation, if they begin at all. Miles of transmission lines must be spread over tough, often unsafe terrain to link these generation facilities to the locations that need the power—an activity that is often economically prohibitive in rural and sparsely populated areas. Without votes to drive electrification, autocracies have often neglected to provide electricity beyond ego-driven projects in capitals. The reliance on centralized grids has left large sections of the developing world literally and figuratively powerless.

Such "powerless" developing countries could provide an ideal market for distributed energy.

Distributed generation is a clear policy winner in the developing world. It keeps countries out of debt, while allowing individuals and villages to sidestep corrupt governments and brittle infra-structure. Unlike the West, the developing world does not need to be reacquainted with distributed energy. Cow-dung patties and scraps of firewood—self-generation based on burning local bio-mass, in energy-speak—continue to fuel rural heating and cook-ing from Indonesia to Equatorial Guinea. But these traditional forms of energy have severe problems. They have made the devel-oping world rife with lung disease, burn injuries, climate damage, and local pollution. Luckily, a host of new forms of distributed energy are already working in the developing world.

Woolsey argued that the developing world's distributed energy projects are already seeing success.

A multitude of distributed generation initiatives already are underway in the developing world, from Kenya, where solar pho-tovoltaic use in rural areas outpaces new grid connections and unsubsidized photovoltaics compose 75 percent of the solar mar-ket, to Inner Mongolia, where China's government has enabled 160,000 herdsmen to draw power from small wind turbines car-ried along with their yurts. Hundreds of pilot projects need to be scaled to enable a broad solution—but they have already shown what is necessary for distributed generation in the developing world to be profitable and sustainable.

Dan Reicher followed Woolsey and said that he had some issues with the term distributed energy, noting that it had become something of a catchall for a variety of different, but sometimes unrelated, concepts.

"Distributed energy" actually is not a very good term because it encompasses virtually everything we want to talk about in the energy world. We do know it is the production of energy close to the location where it will be consumed, but it ranges over a cou-ple orders of magnitude, from watts to megawatts, and a huge range of fuels. The key question is: Is there a significant energy source near the point of use and can we develop that in a cost competitive way?

He noted that some distributed energy sources, such as geothermal, could operate at a scale and consistency far greater than sources such as solar and wind.

> We have a vast resource in geothermal, particularly advanced geothermal energy. Essentially, you drill some distance down, fracture rock, put water down there, bring it back up, create steam, and run a turbine. This is simply exploiting the heat that is in rock at various distances below the surface. This does not suffer from the intermittency problems of solar and wind. So it can, in fact, add a lot from an energy security standpoint.

Reicher noted that such sources could actually operate at enormous scale.

> At a few kilometers, we are looking at tens of thousands of megawatts, at five or six kilometers, hundreds of thousands of megawatts, and at ten kilometers, you're looking literally at millions of megawatts. In California itself, if you only exploited 2 percent of the resource here through enhanced geothermal, you would generate 140,000 megawatts versus its current 63,000 megawatt installed base of generation. That is 2 percent. Now is that a distributed generation source, that kind of power, up and down the state, that close to large population centers? And if you add Nevada into that mix it doubles or triples. That is a huge baseload resource that one might argue is distributed, given that this heat is beneath our feet virtually everywhere.

Reicher also noted that in other areas, technologies such as offshore wind could be promising.

> For tens of miles off the mid-Atlantic coast you can go out and still be in ten meter, twenty meter, thirty meter water. You don't need exotic turbines. This is a vast resource, tens of thousands of megawatts, very close to large population centers. So again, is this a distributed generation opportunity? I don't know. I think so. I think this is a vast one, very close to the major cities of the United States and readily developable.

Reicher noted that his team at Google had sketched out some fairly aggressive possibilities for renewable and alternative energy targets.

> Eliminating coal from the mix, maintaining a fairly significant reliance on natural gas, and moving plug-in vehicles into this mix in a very, very significant way. All the while, we could be creating millions and millions of jobs with very significant net savings to the economy, and 50 percent greenhouse-gas emissions reductions. We are pretty convinced that if you put the right pieces together, you can get pretty far, pretty fast.

He noted that there is a promising federal initiative in this direction, the Clean Energy Development Act (CEDA), proposed by Senate Majority Leader Harry Reid of Nevada.

> One of the challenges we see in clean energy technology is government research and development (R&D). The venture capital community can take technologies to a point where they work at the pilot scale. Tens of millions of dollars have been spent on technology that works at a small scale. The challenge we face—indeed we call it the Valley of Death—is how do we get those first few big commercial projects financed, up and running, and really show that this can work? After that, the mainstream financial community will take over, but it is those first couple of scale-up plants that are a serious problem. CEDA particularly as proposed in the Senate, would do a lot to fix that.

But he added that making a real difference would require a real change in federal attitudes towards energy research, development and deployment (RD&D).

> R&D spending in the federal government is woefully inadequate. President Obama in the campaign talked about 15 to 30 billion dollars a year. We really need to get there, sooner rather than later, if so much of what we need to have happen in this country is going to actually happen. If you put robust R&D together with a really focused federal backing of high-risk deployment—CEDA and R&D spending—we can really drive this world forward in a very significant way.

In response to a question from Paul Berg about establishing an authority with scientific competence within Congress, Reicher expressed a need for change, noting that perhaps the Office of Technology Assessment (OTA) could be reestablished but that the National Academy of Sciences, the National Labs, and the Congressional Research Service served as reasonably good proxies in the interim.

Paul Gipe wondered whether a feed-in tariff had to be done at a federal level. Woolsey said it would more likely happen at a state level but could be encouraged by federal policy.

John Burges noted the critical role that feed-in tariffs had played in building out distributed and renewable energy. "It accounts for over 80 percent of every single solar cell, solar module that's been installed around the world," he said.

Reicher agreed that feed-in tariffs had been useful but felt that they were no substitute for putting a price on carbon in terms of an effect of driving a change in energy usage. Jim Sweeney added that excessive feed-in tariffs presented their own dangers from the standpoint of economic efficiency.

If you have a feed-in tariff with a very high price, you can get investment in a lot of things that are very uneconomical. A lot of the photovoltaics on rooftops are uneconomical in comparison to the result from energy efficiency, so what the feed-in tariff with a high price does is to establish the opportunity and incentive for doing a lot of very uneconomical things while bypassing some of the more economical things.

Woolsey dissented from this view, arguing that feed-in tariffs worked best for businesses with large system installations rather than for individual consumers.

Recommendations

◇ Increase research and development on means of enhancing generation of electricity close to where it is to be used.
◇ Rebuild the national grid so that it can be more easily "islanded," utilizing distributed generation possibilities.
◇ Evaluate the potential for feed-in tariffs.
◇ Support a Clean Energy Deployment Administration to bridge the gap between small-scale demonstrations and full-scale commercial plants.

SESSION 2

What Can We Do To Boost Energy Efficiency?

*"The structure of the energy market makes the invisible
hand not only invisible, but nonexistent. The invisible
hand's just not going to do it for you."*

—JIM SWEENEY

Overview

MEGAWATTS OR NEGAWATTS?—this was the provocative question that energy analyst Amory Lovins asked many years ago.

"Negawatts," or energy efficiency gains that eliminate the need for building new energy infrastructure, has been identified as one of the most promising policies for decreasing energy costs and increasing energy security. California, in particular, has pursued policies for energy efficiency over the past few decades that have kept overall per capita energy consumption flat in the state while it has been soaring nationwide.

Many independent studies suggest that energy efficiency is the most cost-effective method of "generating energy"—but the fact remains that investments in efficiency have been low compared to investments in energy sources. The reasons for this underinvestment have been much debated, as it would seem to violate economists' precepts that people do not, as a rule, leave $20 bills lying on the ground. Part of the reason is opportunity cost and some is knowledge. Part is a question of incentives: utilities are often incentivized to make sure customers use electricity, not conserve it.

It is clear that making progress on energy efficiency relies as much on changing human behavior patterns as it does on technology. Burton Richter remarked that he had run a study for the American Physical Society on energy efficiency. Everybody agreed that should be the number one priority in reducing emissions, and reducing oil imports, and securing our economy, but none knew exactly how to achieve it practically because of behavioral issues, although the panel was able to generate several recommendations of cost-effective strategies.

High oil prices saw energy efficiency programs hit their zenith in the 1970s and first half of the 1980s. The energy efficiency of our economy improved dramatically. When the price of oil dropped in 1985 so did the interest in the programs. Now, with another generation of high fuel prices upon us, and increasing worries about climate change, energy efficiency is again receiving a great deal of attention.

Task Force member Jim Sweeney addressed the Task Force on the subject of energy efficiency. Sweeney, who has been an energy policy scholar for four decades, is one of the nation's leading experts on the subject of energy efficiency. He founded and directs the Precourt Energy Efficiency Center, the leading academic institute in the United States dedicated to studying energy efficiency technologies, policies, and practices. The respondent was Jonathan Koomey, a project scientist at Lawrence Berkeley National Laboratory and a consulting professor at Stanford University who has written eight books and more than 150 articles on various aspects of energy policy, concentrating in particular on energy efficiency.

The Task Force discussed the costs and benefits of efficiency, paying special attention to why, thus far, it had failed to live up to its potential.

There was agreement that both market and behavioral failures drove our energy efficiency challenges. There was agreement that clever market incentives (such as those offered by California) could dramatically boost energy efficiency. There were, however, concerns that such legislation would be economically regressive (the burden would fall to a greater degree on poor taxpayers).

Proceedings

Jim Sweeney began his presentation by defining energy efficiency as "economically efficient reductions in energy use or energy use intensity."

Sweeney argued that we need to make changes in four groups of areas: first, those areas that require new technology and technological development; second, areas where legislation is needed to accomplish results (such as reformed fuel efficiency standards); third, areas where legislation has been proposed but not yet implemented, such as a tax on the damaging uses of energy and smart regional development; and fourth, areas related to human behavior rather than technology or regulation.

Sweeney argued that there are currently two different failures plaguing the energy efficiency sector.

> Two classes of failures to achieve energy efficiency are worth analyzing: market failures and behavioral failures. The market failures are the classic issues that economists have looked at. The

structure of the energy market makes the invisible hand not only invisible, but nonexistent. The invisible hand's just not going to do it for you. As regards behavioral issues, first, most consumers think energy issues have very low salience for them. Put another way: they don't care! And if you say, "Here's a lot of low-cost ways that you could have energy," they say, "Ah, interesting, but I don't really care. A second factor is poor information and lack of cognitive skill necessary to deal with complex issues of costs and benefits of given energy efficiency investments."

Sweeney noted that ultimately solving such problems could prove quite challenging.

The bottom line is there is no reductionist solution that will deal with all of these problems. If you want to have smart policy in energy efficiency, and energy efficiency is where you have the big bang for the buck, you cannot pretend that you just have to do an information strategy, or you just have to do a price strategy, or you just have to do an R&D strategy. We have multiple market and cognitive failures and we have to address them with multiple instruments.

Koomey agreed with Sweeney that there were psychological and knowledge barriers to increasing energy efficiency.

Efficiency does not sell by itself. So if you just make a product more efficient, you are not going to get 90 percent market penetration. We need to think about ways to combine efficiency with other attributes, so that people want them for more than just efficiency.

Koomey also stressed the importance of business organization factors in improving adoption of energy efficiency technologies.

It is important that we become a whole lot more clever about using the power of supply chains. Efficiency products are generally niche products. If you move the niche product, which has a very high markup to become a more commonly used product, the markups come down.

But Koomey was optimistic that cost reductions would solve some of efficiency's business problems in the long run.

Every one and a half years or so, the power use needed to meet a fixed level of computational need goes down by a factor of two. What that means for efficiency is that we will be increasingly able to have real time information and real time control of energy services.

Jim Sweeney suggested that both culture and economics can play a role in creating an environment that is conducive to greater energy efficiency.

We do a lot of things that are energy inefficient relative to what Japan and Europe do. In Europe, there has been a very heavy use of a price signal in gasoline, not particularly because they wanted a price signal, but because that was a good source of revenue for the European governments who are always looking at creative ways to raise revenue. But if you go to Japan, there is a very different cultural attitude about saving versus wasting. So there is a group of cultural attitudes, some of which are influenced by economics, some of which are influenced by education, that play a role here.

In response to Koomey and Sweeney's comments, Task Force chair George Shultz stressed the importance of culture in making a transformation to greater energy efficiency.

The cultural component that has been mentioned is very powerful. Nobody claims that prices determine everything, although it is certainly true that price signals are reacted to very strongly. But there is a lot of room for other measures in this field.

As you are trying to get people to use energy more effectively and efficiently, certainly it is key to get the price signals right. But then on top of that, it can be useful to say, "Look how stupid you are to use your washing machine at midday when you can use it at 10:00 in the evening and save money." All these little things, they make a difference over time. This approach is common practice in any corporate setting. The way you manage things is in part by the price signals but also by instilling a culture.

Sweeney agreed with Shultz.

The message to leave with people is that when we deal with energy efficiency, there are a lot of things that we have to pay attention to that go beyond the technology and the economics. The failure to completely grasp this is one of the reasons why the low hanging fruit has not been picked.

Tara Billingsley asked about the potential economic regressivity of some of the proposed policies and their extensions—particularly a cap-and-trade carbon policy to reduce emissions. Sweeney agreed that distribution of gains and losses from such policies is an issue but felt that it could be handled effectively through good policy design.

As it turns out, you can have a cap-and-trade system and then say, "We recognize that people in the bottom, some fraction of the population, will be financially disadvantaged." And you can very directly try to deal with that. You can deal with that through community development programs if you think it is going to be a community-based way of doing it. In California, through our electric utilities systems, we have a group of safety net programs that allow low-income people to get subsidies on their electricity. The fact that you have to do something else to deal with potential inequities should never be a reason for not getting good instruments in place. Separately, you can see how you can deal with these other problems.

Recommendations

In the United States, improvements in energy efficiency can be made at the state and local level, as the state of California has shown. A national energy efficiency policy should encourage leadership by the private sector and by state and local governments. This effort should be supported at all levels of government by the following actions:

- Provide easily accessible information regarding energy pricing and consumption and how to reduce consumption while preserving the benefits that energy conveys;
- Package energy-efficient products with other useful and attractive features so that incentives to buy such products are enhanced;
- Increase the use of information technology to support efficient use of energy;
- Adopt standards at the federal, state, and local levels to enhance energy efficiency, for example, in building codes.

SESSION 3

The Nuclear Fuel Cycle

*"We will not know for decades the full extent of the
demand for nuclear fuel due to expansion of nuclear
energy. Nor will we know the availability of the uranium
resource that can be recovered at reasonable cost. Nor will
we know which technologies will become available to
overcome the economic and proliferation drawbacks of
reprocessing as practiced today."*

—ELLEN TAUSCHER

Overview

PRESIDENT DWIGHT EISENHOWER spoke about the dilemma
of atomic energy in his address to the United Nations on December 8, 1953: "The United States pledges before you . . . its deter-
mination to help solve the fearful atomic dilemma—to devote its
entire heart and mind to finding the way by which the miracu-
lous inventiveness of man shall not be dedicated to his death,
but consecrated to his life."

The dilemma is that the same technology that can provide
energy to a world badly in need of it can also be used to

construct the most devastating weapons that have ever been invented. The production of enriched uranium and separation of plutonium from spent fuel from nuclear power plants, or reactors, provide the materials needed to build an atomic bomb. The technology required to construct a rudimentary nuclear weapon is now widely available.

Although these problems are technical in nature, the challenge of preventing civil nuclear power programs from being used for weapons purposes is essentially political and economic in nature. Denying technology to countries that lack it has been difficult to do consistently. The states that agreed in the Nonproliferation Treaty to renounce nuclear weapons programs have been reluctant to accept an inferior status in civil nuclear power. The states possessing nuclear weapons have faced commercial pressures to transfer technology and have had a tendency to bend the rules for friends and allies. A level playing field has been hard to create.

During the administration of George W. Bush, the U.S. proposed an international agreement to ban the transfer of uranium enrichment and plutonium processing technology to nations that do not already have such facilities. This was rejected out of hand by almost all nations. Even some modest, criteria-based guidelines for transfers have been opposed by countries that saw a market for supplying enriched uranium. At the same time, the Bush administration negotiated a deal with India that made that country an exception to the rules of the Nonproliferation Treaty and pressured other nations to endorse it. The jury is still out on whether the Nuclear Suppliers Group can agree on conditions for technology transfers that meet today's demands for a level playing field and an end to the two-tier system of states in the civil nuclear field.

Powerful economic incentives exist that should persuade nations to forgo building facilities for producing enriched uranium and for separating plutonium. The capital costs are very high and the frequency of use is fairly low. This fact is perhaps the best hope for curtailing the spread of nationally owned and operated facilities. To encourage this economically rational outcome and provide assurances of a reliable flow of fuel cycle services, the United States and other countries have proposed nuclear fuel "banks" on which countries requiring nuclear fuels could draw if they encountered difficulties in securing fuel through normal commercial markets. Proposals have been advanced for the multilateralization of uranium enrichment facilities by including more than one country in the ownership and/or operation of these facilities. So far, the normal operations of commercial markets has sufficed for those nations that see atomic power as part of a mix of energy sources and are content to remain dependent on outside supplies. The fuel bank and multilateral production facilities have not been utilized very extensively. Those countries that have decided to opt for national uranium enrichment faculties have done so, in all probability, to create options for manufacturing a nuclear weapon, as well as to maintain their independence from outside suppliers for their energy needs.

The "back end" of the nuclear fuel cycle poses the question of what to do with nuclear fuel after it has been irradiated in reactors. It can be reprocessed to extract plutonium for nuclear weapons. It can be processed so that the plutonium content can be recycled as fuel in reactors, fast neutron reactors among them. Or it can be processed so that the plutonium is essentially unusable by embedding the spent fuel material in vitreous "logs." In the United States, most of the used fuel has been deposited in cooling ponds adjacent to the reactors where the fuel rods were irradiated. And there it has sat, with no agreement on what to do with it next in many cases because a long-term depository acceptable to the communities surrounding it could not be found. The option of the Yucca Mountain depository in Nevada has been discarded by the Obama administration. This underscores the inability of generations of American political leaders to solve the problem of used fuel disposition.

The impasse has been exacerbated by U.S. legislation that makes it difficult to receive used fuel from foreign-based reactors. The overall effect of these political attitudes and policies has been to affect adversely nonproliferation interests. The United States has not been able to offer assurances to nations that might be willing to buy U.S. reactors and fuel them with leased fuel elements from the United States that the used fuel would be taken back by the United States. This has reduced American ability to exert influence over transactions that have nuclear proliferation implications.

The Energy Task Force invited Ellen Tauscher, undersecretary of state for arms control and international security to discuss some of the most important issues in this area. Tauscher, who for many years represented in Congress a portion of the San Francisco Bay Area that includes the National Laboratory at Livermore, has been a longtime leader in nuclear policy. The discussion was moderated by Robert Rosner, former director of the Argonne National Laboratory and a lead expert in nuclear policy. The discussant was Tom Isaacs of the Center for International Security and Cooperation (CISAC) at Stanford. Isaacs spent more than two decades at the Department of Energy in a variety of senior roles related to nuclear energy, and he has continued that work today at CISAC and Lawrence Livermore National Laboratory.

In the ensuing discussion, questions arose regarding the economic viability of nuclear reactors, particularly in light of the new findings concerning reserves of natural gas. Participants engaged in debate concerning the extent to which the United States should encourage or discourage the development of nuclear power options in sensitive parts of the world. The desirability of burning plutonium in light-water reactors in order to reduce the amount of plutonium was also raised and discussed.

Proceedings

Tauscher introduced some important new initiatives related to the nuclear fuel cycle and nuclear security. She asserted that new storage programs were critical.

> What we are looking for is placement of used fuel in a storage facility for fifty to one hundred years with the ability to retrieve it at any time. From a technical point of view, dry cask technology is proven and licensed and available for this purpose.

But Tauscher was quick to point out that there are many uncertainties that plague this process.

> We will not know for decades the full extent of the demand for nuclear fuel due to expansion of nuclear energy. Nor will we know the availability of the uranium resource that can be recovered at reasonable cost. Nor will we know which technologies will become available to overcome the economic and proliferation drawbacks of reprocessing as practiced today.

She stressed the importance of building interim storage capacity while the longer-term options were sorted out.

> Retrievable interim storage would preserve options for future decisions when we have the information necessary to make informed choices on what to do with used fuel.

She also said the United States is willing to play a leading role in facilitating interim storage for countries without the capacity to do so.

> The question becomes where to store used fuel. Part of the answer is in the same country—usually at the same site—where the fuel was irradiated. The United States and others can assist a country seeking nuclear energy in implementing a safe, secure, and economical system for interim storage on the reactor site, or elsewhere in that country.

Tauscher noted that Russia was currently taking back used fuel but could not expect to take on this responsibility alone, nor would the potential leverage Russia would obtain over new reactor sales be in the U.S. interest. The Russians only take used fuel from Russian-built reactors. Tauscher argued that it may well be in U.S. interests to take back used fuel from some reactors that it sells abroad.

> One can argue that it would be in the interest of the United States and other suppliers of reactor technology and fuel to take back used fuel for storage. At present, bringing to the United States used fuel irradiated in nuclear power plants abroad requires notification of Congress, which would almost certainly lead to Congressional opposition to such imports. While the odds are against us, we could work with Congress to seek an ability to offer interim storage of used fuel from abroad, for countries that do not have sensitive fuel-cycle facilities.

The guiding concept was summed up as follows.

> Establishment of regional or international interim storage facilities could make an important contribution to an attractive offer for countries considering nuclear energy. Used fuel could be stored at the reactor site for a period of time, followed by storage at an international facility, followed by a decision on ultimate disposition.

Moderator Robert Rosner agreed with Tauscher.

> Nuclear power does matter, and the way it is deployed internationally matters. The back end of the fuel cycle matters much more than it has been given credence for before. The fiction that we do not have interim storage needs to stop. We need to recognize that we have had interim storage all along; we have just called it storage at the nuclear reactor sites. We need action now, but one of the things we should not do is reprocess light-water reactor fuel. That would be a huge mistake now. International action is required now, not just in a narrow area but in the complete nuclear fuel cycle, including such things as economic incentives, mechanisms like the international fuel banks and take-back provisions. This requires three things, in my view, on the part of the United States. One is leadership, which I think we are showing, it requires collegiality, and for a change we're showing that, and it requires consistency. It remains to be seen whether we will show consistency. We have not been outstanding on that.

He also said that U.S. technology in the nuclear field was falling behind and that this was both a long-term commercial failure and a potential security risk.

We have been losing technical competence and technical credibility in nuclear power for the past two decades. This is especially so, unfortunately, on the back end. We have severely constrained take-back provisions. Currently, we do not sell nuclear reactors. The folks who are selling nuclear reactors are foreign-owned companies. We are losing our technological competence on the front end, on the back end, and in the middle. How can we actually be leaders in this context? What do we do about that?

Isaacs suggested several steps that the United States should take.

One, we need to work to provide nuclear power at market prices and maybe even assist countries into entry in the nuclear power market. Two, we need to assure fuel supplies through a healthy marketplace and through other kinds of fuel assurances, such as fuel banks. Three, we need to eliminate incentives and rationales for enrichment and reprocessing plants except for a select few that are under international aegis and control. Four, we need a program to secure all weapons-usable material that is excess: today there are 250 metric tons of separated civilian plutonium around the world and it is growing. We are separating plutonium faster than we are using it. We need to draw down that material to as close to zero as possible in as few places as possible. We also need to ensure that any moves toward weapons or the acquisition of weapons-usable materials are surely, quickly, and clearly apparent so that the fig leaf of energy adequacy and economic development is removed.

Isaacs said that the back end of the fuel cycle is the critical piece to manage.

We need to see if we can not use the back end of the fuel cycle and its potential provision of storage and, ultimately, disposal, as a way to provide for a set of norms that provide security, energy, and waste management services better than we are meeting all of them today. I believe the back end is the linchpin.

Isaacs echoed Tauscher's suggestion that the United States could play a larger role in international fuel management and disposal.

Where other countries surely will need help, from the moment they start up a reactor, is in the back end because, as we have been talking about, storage is tough—it is not so tough technically, it is very tough politically. Disposal is very expensive; it makes no sense. Half the countries in the world today that have nuclear power have five or fewer reactors. It makes no sense for those countries or newly emerging nuclear nations to all go through the agony and the economic penalty of each building its own repository.

He concluded by saying that such disposal must be regional in nature to be most effective.

So, regional storage and, ultimately, regional disposal can lead to a win-win situation. The tough part is, of course, where do you put it? And there, I believe, we are learning more and more by experience you just have to find the right situation where one or two or three countries find it in their own self-interest to do these kinds of things. You can change the dynamic. If Russia or some other country starts to say, "We'll provide the reactor and we'll take care of the spent fuel; we'll take it back or it will go to a third country in a takeaway circumstance as part of the bargain. You don't have to worry about the spent fuel. You don't have to worry about the disposal." That may change the dynamic very, very quickly and we may see competition for that service, because it is a service that can be provided relatively straightforwardly and safely if you can deal with the institutional issues.

Recommendations

◊ The coupling of the likely expansion of nuclear power globally with the absolutely essential task of trying to rid the world of nuclear weapons suggests that this is the time to act to bring the nuclear fuel cycle under control.

◊ A four-pronged approach to the unresolved problem of how to handle spent fuel should be pursued:

1. research, in association with international partners, on how to develop reactors that would avoid the necessity of separating plutonium or have the potential for high burn-up of uranium and plutonium;

2. work to create interim storage facilities for used fuel with the ability to retrieve the fuel at any time;

3. develop "cradle to the grave" fuel services including fuel leasing and take-back options;

4. continue to look for locations and methods for permanent disposal of spent fuel.

SESSION 4

Synthetic Biology and Its Applications in Energy

"This is some of the most powerful technology ever developed by humans. It rivals nuclear technology because it can be done by a few individuals with simple tools. So the policy cannot be just to let us alone."

—CRAIG VENTER

Overview

SYNTHETIC BIOLOGY is the name for an emerging scientific discipline that aims to use living organisms, most frequently microorganisms, to perform the most complicated chemical syntheses. This wholly novel approach to making complex and often rare chemicals emerged from the developments of the recombinant DNA technology in the 1970s and 1980s. Then, molecular biologists learned how to isolate genes in pure form from virtually any living and even dead organism and to propagate them in a variety of microbes and animal cells. Subsequently, biochemists, microbiologists, molecular biologists, and geneticists, and the biotech companies they spawned, showed that genes could be programmed to produce commercially valuable and critical

43

pharmaceuticals on an industrial scale. Emerging from those advances was the recognition that the molecules and the basic mechanisms of cellular processes are virtually identical or closely related in all forms of life on our planet. We know that genes are made of a complex chemical referred to as DNA. Remarkably, the structure and constituents of DNAs are identical regardless of what organism they come from. Moreover, genes can be synthesized rather easily and quickly in the laboratory with widely available automated machines.

We also know that genes are the source of information to produce all the proteins made by cells and that proteins are the catalysts for the myriad metabolic and synthetic processes carried out by living cells. Proteins are also chemicals, and they too can be made in the laboratory. The synthetic biologist is not constrained to deal with genes and proteins as they exist in nature; they can be readily modified to alter their functions to suit particular purposes. Molecular biologists can isolate genes or collections of genes from even the most mundane or exotic organisms and, after some optimization, they can be translated into proteins in another suitable organism. It is this power that encourages synthetic biologists to undertake the creation of "designer microbes" by modifying existing genes or creating new ones that enable such organisms to perform novel functions or to produce otherwise hard-to-come-by molecules. The most ambitious goal is to make wholly synthetic microbes whose genomes endow them with "tailor-made" desirable capabilities.

In seeking to make biological systems easy to build, synthetic biologists have adopted a strategy modeled after the computer industry. For example, a computer chip may be considered as a collection of microcircuits assembled on a common support to perform a discrete function. Depending on how such assemblies are organized they can create very distinct complex programs, each with a wide variety of functions. Thus, modular subassemblies of genes that carry out specific functions are used to produce more complex assemblies. Pursuing that model, a collection of different gene modules can be mixed in various combinations for novel and special applications.

The field of synthetic biology is in its infancy, but it is grounded in the application of engineering principles to the existing knowledge and experience of molecular biology. As the number of sequenced genomes increase and the libraries of individual genes are enlarged, we can expect to expand the ways simple organisms or even wholly synthetic organisms will be designed to serve human needs. Deliberatively designed plants, animals, and microbes may become the factories of the future. Nevertheless, we need to acknowledge that nothing in the man-made world rivals the complexity and diversity of living things or of the information systems that determine their properties. Current ignorance is vaster than current knowledge. There are in nature, remaining to be discovered, concepts that no one has yet imagined. And we can expect that the speeding pace of technology will create opportunities that dwarf our present ambitions.

Last year the Royal Academy of Engineering in the United Kingdom issued a report saying the new approaches of synthetic biology have a chance to be the transformative technology of this next century. It is likely to be the major source of wealth generation for nations, really transforming what can be done and limited right now mostly by our imaginations.

The federal government, with the support of the scientific community, has created oversight mechanisms to provide guidance regarding safety and security issues. Three of the most important are as follows:

- The Recombinant DNA Advisory Committee (RAC) was established on October 7, 1974. It operated under the aegis of the National Institutes of Health.
- On March 28, 2008, the National Science Advisory Board for Biosecurity was created. Its mission is to provide biosecurity oversight of dual-use research. Its advice is provided to the secretary of health and human services, the director of the National Institutes of Health, and to the heads of all federal departments and agencies that conduct or support life science research.
- The National Academy of Sciences/National Research Council establishes committees from time to time to investigate safety and security issues. These typically address specific questions and issue reports. They have no continuing oversight responsibilities.

The Energy Task Force is particularly interested in the possible applications of synthetic biology to energy, which is one of the most promising early markets for synthetic biology products. The Energy Task Force was fortunate to have many of the leaders of this emerging discipline on hand for its discussion of this subject. Several of our panelists have been involved with research into next generation biofuels and other energy processes that take advantage of developments in synthetic biology.

The session moderator, Paul Berg, is a pioneer in the synthetic biology field and a Nobel laureate in chemistry. Much of this overview is drawn from a presentation he made to the Energy Task Force. The presentation speaker, Craig Venter, is CEO of Synthetic Genomics and the leader of the first successful effort to sequence the human genome. Joining as panelists were Jay Keasling, director of the Physical Biosciences Division, Lawrence Berkeley Lab, and director of the Synthetic Biology Engineering Research Center. Keasling is also CEO of the U.S.

Department of Energy's Joint Bioenergy Institute and a professor in the Department of Chemical Engineering at the University of California, Berkeley. The final discussant was Drew Endy, an assistant professor of Bioengineering at Stanford University, the founder of the BioBricks initiative, and a pioneer in the field of synthetic biology.

The discussion ranged over possible applications, the need for basic research funding, security concerns, and appropriate governmental responses. There was wide agreement on the importance of increasing government funding, particularly for basic research into synthetic biology fundamentals. There was shared concern about potential intellectual property issues in the sector and the possible environmental damage from accidents. There was also agreement that security concerns would need to be addressed in a meaningful way to gain public trust, though there was disagreement about the validity of some of those security concerns. There was some dispute about the uniqueness of synthetic biology in addressing some of the issues of liquid fuels, and some participants also sounded a cautionary note about addressing energy problems through synthetic biology without paying sufficient attention to research fundamentals.

Proceedings

Craig Venter began by discussing his own work in synthetic genomics, an emerging frontier in synthetic biology.

> Essentially, we start with a digital code in the computer. We write new software, the software of life, a genetic code. By doing so, we can actually create totally new life forms that have not existed

before. What we have been doing for the last few decades is digitizing biology. When we read the genetic codes, we take the four-letter chemical code and convert it to ones and zeros in the computer.

He noted that recent advances in synthetic genomics had meant that research development and applications could be accelerated.

Now we can go from ones and zeros in the computer without any human intervention into making a wide range of pieces of DNA. We are working on building a robot that will do this automatically.

Venter noted that the potential new synthetic biology technologies were transformative.

We have totally gone across the boundaries of life. In most bacteria, the genomes can not be easily modified, but in yeast we have a whole spectrum of tools that allow very rapid modification. So we can modify things in yeast, methylate the chromosome if necessary, and transplant it into a new bacterial cell transforming that into a new species.

Venter said that his company's researchers had designed new "software of life" to create new species for defined purposes. He noted that current developments he was working on had particular import for energy and that while creating liquid fuel from algae used to be considered "a farming problem" (that is, How do you grow enough of it?), this was no longer the case.

We engineered a cell to do something a lot more exciting. As it makes the lipids, it just pumps them out in a continuous fashion. This now changes fuel production, oil production, food production to biomanufacturing versus farming.

Venter said that major energy industry players were beginning to take note of the potential of synthetic biology.

> Last summer Exxon announced a starting investment of $600 million to really scale up algae/CO_2 to fuel on a grand scale. It is going to be three to four square miles. If we cannot produce fuel in the billions of gallons, it is not worth doing. Most of the things going on with algae are people playing, not really trying to get to this new scale. Also, with BP, we have a program looking at microorganisms for converting coal and other hydrocarbons into at least slightly cleaner substances.

Jay Keasling built on Venter's discussion of the potential energy uses of synthetic biology by describing some of his own research in this area. He said that 1.3 billion tons of biomass goes unutilized every year in the United States and that much of this biomass has the potential to be converted into fuels.

> The energy in that biomass is roughly equivalent to the energy in the amount of oil we produce domestically every year. So with that billion tons of biomass we have the potential to replace the domestic production of oil.

Keasling was critical of the current U.S. approach to biofuels on both efficiency and cost grounds.

> Currently in the United States we produce fuels, primarily ethanol, from corn and that means from starch. Corn is a great food crop, but it was never intended to be an energy crop. It requires a lot of water and a great deal of fertilizer. The production of fertilizer is a huge consumer of energy.

Most energy analysts believe that corn ethanol is a net energy loser and also not cost efficient.

Keasling said that synthetic biology offered a radically better approach to biofuel production.

> By degrading biomass and turning it into a sugar, a microbe can then consume it and turn it into a fuel. Ethanol can be used in low percentages as an oxygenate in gasoline; special automobiles are needed to use it at a higher percentage. You need a completely different infrastructure to use it as a 100 percent fuel. It can not be piped through our traditional pipelines because it is corrosive. And it takes a lot of energy to distill ethanol out of a fermentation broth. In contrast, the beauty of producing things like biodiesel or biojet is that we can engineer the microbe to excrete these. They go out of the cell and they float to the top, you can skim them off and, if it is the molecule you want, you put it in your tank. There is no expensive distillation process.

Keasling talked about the structure of his synthetic biology work and the growing national collaboration on synthetic biology issues. He noted that his Synthetic Biology Engineering Research Center brings together synthetic biologists from UC Berkeley, University of California, San Francisco, Stanford, Harvard University, and the Massachusetts Institute of Technology. The consortium is working together to produce new fuels such as biogasoline, biojet fuel, and biodiesel.

Drew Endy's comments followed Keasling's, and he suggested looking beyond synthetic-biology driven fuel production.

> It may not be the case that bioenergy by itself will solve our problems. We have to recognize that we are going to need a lot more from biology.

Endy cited the importance of synthetic biologists thinking in terms of not just creating fuels but of how we could use synthetic biology to solve energy-related problems.

Thirty years ago Genencor modified a protein that is used in a laundry detergent so that you can wash your clothes in cold water. That enables more people to do their laundry at cold water temperatures, which means that you do not have to burn so much oil to heat your water. The gross impact of that was estimated to be about a hundred thousand barrels of oil a day circa 1980. One of the lessons is not to focus only on making fuels but to think very clearly about how we could integrate biotechnology throughout human civilization in order to reduce our energy needs and solve that problem broadly.

Endy said that the big problem in the field was that scientists need to engage more with the public on the implications of synthetic biology, both in energy and in other fields as well.

We have not yet seen the development of very strong public technical leadership. The opportunities to provide strong leadership in the development of some of these new tools are unbelievable. It would be wonderful to explore whether or not that might be practical and, if it is, how to do it.

The conversation continued with questions from the audience. Lucy Shapiro felt that more fundamental work had to be done in the area of basic research.

We are assuming that we understand fully the cells that we are putting genetic constructs into, but the point is we do not. It is going to become absolutely essential that we understand the inherent genetic circuitry that simple cells use to incorporate genes, to make them respond to our bidding and have them do more complicated things that we are not even envisioning as yet. So my question is: How can we support the very, very basic fundamental work, the fundamental research that must go hand-in-hand with the utterly remarkable stuff that we have heard about this morning?

Venter agreed but said that as the knowledge of the remarkable practical applications become widely known, support for fundamental work would increase.

Task Force chair George Shultz asked about what the best public policy framework would be from the perspective of research scientists. Venter noted that right now there was very little funding from the government for basic synthetic biology research and that most of the funding had come from the medical and petrochemical industries. Nonetheless, he acknowledged the importance of a larger government role going forward, including regulatory standards that would prevent abuse and the potential creation of dangerous organisms.

> This is some of the most powerful technology ever developed by humans. It rivals nuclear technology because it can be done by a few individuals with simple tools. So the policy cannot be just to let us alone. We do not want kids to be the first ones on their block to build the Ebola virus in their garage. Smallpox is about a quarter of the size of the molecules we can make in a relatively short period of time. So the biosecurity side is a very critical part of this.

Venter stressed that it was important to monitor these developments and begin designing intelligent regulations now, rather than letting a sudden event dictate policy.

> Any powerful technology today, no matter what it is, is in this new category that the National Academy calls dual-use technology. We need intelligent monitoring of this. Congress made it a capital offense to make smallpox but that has actually thwarted a lot of research by people trying to make smallpox vaccines. So we need to be smart about how we do things and not have knee-jerk responses. Right now the U.S. government is not involved at all other than sort of watching what happens.

Moving to the issue of particular energy uses of synthetic biology, Task Force member Jim Woolsey disagreed on the importance of replacing traditional corn-based ethanol with a synthetic biology alternative.

> Corn-based ethanol is not the invention of the devil. The protein
> in an ethanol plant goes through the system, is dried, and the
> residue comes out the other end so that cattle still get the protein.
> What is taken away from them and turned into fuel for vehicles,
> lessening our requirement for oil, is the corn starch. One does not
> need to shoot down other ways, however imperfect, of moving us
> away from petroleum.

But Venter disagreed with this assessment of corn-based ethanol.

> There are a lot of reasons to shoot down corn-based ethanol.
> Number one, talking about policy, Congress mandated corn-
> based ethanol at the expense of any other solutions to biofuels. It
> doubled the cost of feed and the cost of food when fuel prices
> were high. Using food land and food crops for producing energy
> is just a dumb policy when there are alternatives. We could
> replace basically the entire oil transportation industry for the
> world with an algae facility twice the size of Maryland. If they
> tried to do that with corn-based ethanol, it would take something
> like five times the size of the United States.

Task Force member Andy Karsner took up the issue of government involvement.

> What is being said is not that the government is not involved but
> that it is involved insufficiently and is not organized in the right
> way. For our forum's purposes we would like to understand how
> the government with minimal touch can organize itself suffi-
> ciently to affect scaling and integration into the economy of some

of the applications that you have mentioned? Two examples stand out: liquid fuel's substitution at a rate and scale that are consequential; and CO_2 conversion from waste streams into value streams. Those two things are at the core of everything we are talking about.

Venter noted that the Department of Energy (DOE) had funded early work but that there had been reluctance on DOE's part to fund biological research as it was out of their area of expertise.

Venter said that the point was that fuels created with synthetic biology could be similar or identical to existing fuels.

> We do not have to invent something radically new to make cost-effective fuels. There is a point in trying to use fuels that fit into the existing infrastructure. So the plan we have with Exxon is to take our biocrude right out of these biomanufacturing facilities into their refineries to make gasoline, diesel, jet fuel, etc. The biocrude would not be distinguishable from existing fuels except by a chemist.

But he noted that one challenge in developing biocrude and other new energy technologies with synthetic biology was that there were still very few experts globally in the field.

> There are a lot of different aspects to this because this is new. The science is new. The policies are new. These directions are new. You're looking at 50 percent of the scientific community leading this effort at this table.

Paul Berg agreed and argued that training grants might offer the best return for invested dollar.

> This is a game-changer. The question is how do we fund the game-changers to derive full benefit from them?

Endy argued against a sole focus on energy in developing the technology.

> Getting crisp, sustained policy driven by energy needs, so that investments in bioenergy are sustained and investments in tools that are the game-changers are included, would be fantastic. However, if we only drove this with energy it would be a first-order mistake. Foundational understanding needs to get integrated into this. The potential for this technology to impact how we manufacture things and how we understand ourselves and the living world is so profound that if we only drive our policy via energy, we are going to miss something real big.

Endy argued that several categories of investments and developments needed to take place.

> First, we need public investments in tools and foundational science. Getting better at building genetic material should be a national strategic priority. Second, we need policy help and partners specifically on two topics: security and property rights. The security issue arises when people outside your community intend to cause harm. That is something that a scientific community or an engineering community cannot handle alone. And property rights policies probably need to be updated. When semiconductors really took off, Intel and other U.S. manufacturers had to lead Congress through a new piece of property rights legislation. When we start putting together thousands and tens of thousands of genetic components into engineered organisms, a patent-based property rights framework alone is not going to cut it. It is too slow and it is too expensive and it does not scale. We are going to need something that is leaner and has a lower transaction cost.

In response to Burton Richter's query on where new policies should focus, Venter stressed that security is, to his mind, most important.

I think the number one thing the government needs to focus on is security. The best way to focus on security is not by licensing things and tying things up and limiting what students and others can do. If anything, government could initiate crash programs for new antivirals and antimicrobials and new vaccines. Then, if new infections emerge, whether they are from some crackpot making something synthetically or from our population that is going to keep growing, we will have solutions for it.

Endy felt that more funding for foundational tools was the most critical need, an approach that was heartily agreed to by Keasling.

It is relatively easy to attract the funding for applications for energy, for health, but to my knowledge the only grant that has been given for the development of foundational tools is to the Synthetic Biology Engineering Research Center and that is on the order of $20 million, funding about twenty investigators. And that is $20 million spread over a five-year period. So investments in the foundations of synthetic biology, which are really going to create the next Silicon Valley, just are not there.

Venter said the problem did not exist as much in the legislature as in the scientific bureaucracy itself.

It is not a problem with Congress. It is a problem with the institutes not even asking Congress for the money for that. You cannot legislate creativity. You cannot just throw money out there and expect it to happen. These ideas have to percolate out and develop.

Tara Billingsley said that as someone working on legislation, more clarity was needed on the future production from the scientific community.

We are currently at a crossroads because what we have right now in the renewable fuel area is ethanol. We need to decide what we are going to do about the infrastructure challenge that ethanol presents. We need some sort of read on how far we should go to integrate ethanol into the existing fuel supply versus waiting for a drop-in fuel industry.

Keasling replied that drop-in fuels would be available within five years, and therefore more money should not be spent on ethanol infrastructure.

Venter argued that the scale of the synthetic biology fuels investment needed to be massive.

We need to create billions of gallons of fuel per facility for years. Otherwise we are just playing. It is going to take on the order of ten years to have the first of those facilities with the current level of investments. These are going to be multibillion-dollar facilities. So they are not going to be built with biotech or venture capital funding. It would be built either with the Exxons, the BPs, and the other fuel giants of the world, and/or with government funding. Perhaps it can happen faster, but the engineering is more limiting than the biology is right now.

Venter further expanded on environmental and security concerns.

I get asked frequently about inadvertent environmental damage. We certainly have to be concerned with that. No small part of our oxygen atmosphere comes from processes involving algae in the ocean and we certainly do not want to have noncontrollable modified or synthetic algae in open pond systems that could easily get out in the environment. They have suicide genes in them. They have chemical dependencies. One of the tenets we observe is that organisms we are building must be engineered to have multiple levels so they could not possibly survive in the environment. But if rules like that are not adopted universally by the scientific community, then one major contamination could ruin a whole industry.

He also expressed concern that the United States was not keeping up in research competition with Asia.

The Japanese government has put several billion dollars into this field already. India and China are moving very aggressively across the board. I mean it went from zero in the genomics field to the largest genome facility by about two orders of magnitude over the rest of the combined facilities in the West. The wealth generation of future OPECs is going to be created by countries very different from those that control oil today. The competition is fierce, and if we do not get going in this country, we are going to pay a huge set of prices for it in the future. That is far more important than biosecurity.

Endy said that dramatic gains needed to be made in intellectual property protection.

For the scale of things that are going to be deployed and where investment is needed, it is absolutely critical to have very strong property rights protection. You will not find the investments materializing without something like patents. If we can get to a future where there is a mixture of technology platforms—some very powerful and professional and proprietary—and others open and free to use, we will see a much more vibrant biotechnology industry. So we need a mix and it is worth considering what a new type of property rights might look like in a world where the digitization of biology is taking place.

Keasling echoed this assessment.

> For the project where we were engineering microbes to develop the antimalarial drug, we had to specifically avoid using components that had patents that would require licenses, because we could not afford to produce an inexpensive antimalarial drug and still pay license fees for all the components we were going to need. But on the other hand, we needed to patent the organism that produced the antimalarial drug so that we would not be blocked in using the technology. We need some mixture of proprietary and open. But open-source, free-to-use components would be fabulous for projects in the developing world.

Paul Berg closed the session with a plea for openness.

> We should not want to hinder research or encourage every institution to guard the most trivial kinds of operations. End products, novel end products, which serve a real commercial need can be patented. The tools that we use to make them ought to be open.

Recommendations

Funding

◊ Although "bottom-up" research and development initiatives are the most likely route to innovation, "top-down" guidance from the federal level also is needed. This should take the form of setting national goals in the synthetic biology field so that funding could be coordinated around those broad goals. Incentives, such as prizes, should be built into the system.

◊ Federal funding for foundational research in synthetic biology is needed if the United States is to take full benefit of the national wealth-generation potential of this field and avoid inadvertent events that could cause environmental and safety problems.

◊ Synthetic biology is inherently an interdisciplinary science and this must be recognized in the approach federal funding agencies adopt in their support for foundational research. Improved coordination among these agencies (DOE, Department of Defense, National Institutes of Health) is urgently needed. R&D support is much too piecemeal today.

Safety and Security

◊ Several mechanisms have been created at the federal and university levels over the years to ensure the highest standards of safety and security (see discussion in text). The mandates of these mechanisms should be reviewed and updated so that research and development, as well as commercial applications, including containment procedures, can be more effectively monitored, and in a timely way.

◊ Innovation is inherently the result of unfettered scientific enquiry and this must be encouraged, if only so that the United States can maintain its technological edge. At the same time, there is an inescapable element of unpredictability in such work, and this needs to be taken into account both in funding and in monitoring activities in this field ("DNA shuffling" is an example of a technique that has potentially dangerous consequences). Research into more effective and lower cost vaccines is desirable, partly as a safeguard against the threat or use of pathogens created by sub-state entities.

Property Rights

⋄ A mix of proprietary rights and free, open access to information in the synthetic biology field is the best way to encourage research while creating incentives for entrepreneurs and investors. The dividing line should be drawn between the end products, which should be patented, and the tools used to make them, which should be open to promote further innovation and development.

Public Support

⋄ A dialogue with the public is needed in order to explain more fully and clearly what synthetic biology can offer to the economy and to quality of life. This should avoid "overbranding" and hyperbole and should explain what is being done both to advance the science and to deal with the unintended consequences.

SESSION 5

Putting a Price on Carbon

"But if I put on the hat of a pragmatic economist and say, 'Look, it might be a long time before one could get the ideal policy' then I might say, 'Well, now it is beginning to look like cap-and-trade or at least the hybrid is something to go for.'"

—LARRY GOULDER

Overview

Burning any fossil fuel creates carbon dioxide, the gas widely believed by scientists to be the principal culprit in global climate change. For this reason, any energy policy that is serious about addressing the issue of global climate change must, either directly or indirectly, put a price on carbon. Such carbon pricing can be accomplished in a variety of ways: through a direct "carbon tax" or a "cap-and-trade" scheme or even a "cap and dividend" or revenue-neutral carbon tax in which any net revenues gained from the tax flow back to consumers through a reduction of other taxes or by other means.

Such measures are, of course, not without controversy. Either a carbon tax or a cap-and-trade system effectively raises the price of most commercial energy in the United States, which is derived from fossil fuels. The political advantage to a cap-and-trade over a carbon tax is that it imposes a tax in a less obvious manner. But as political opponents were quick to note, cap-and-trade effectively serves the same purpose as a carbon tax. Opponents of this policy have consistently branded cap-and-trade as "cap-and-tax" and have opposed it with as much vigor as they presumably would have opposed any tax increase.

The primary structural differences between a carbon tax and cap-and-trade are that, in its pure form, a carbon tax limits the actual amount of emissions indirectly by raising the price to a known level, while a cap-and-trade sets a strict amount of allowable emissions but gives no guarantees to emitters on the price of abatement. As was apparent from the Task Force's discussion of the issue, however, the reality of implementation is not so simple.

Economists generally prefer a more straightforward tax to a pure cap-and-trade system, which many economists feel is more susceptible to market manipulation by market players or speculators. In the introduction, Task Force chair George Shultz argued for a revenue-neutral carbon tax, feeling that the issue of climate change should not be used as a pretext for raising taxes.

But Shultz argued that the distinctions between carbon tax and cap-and-trade were sometimes overblown:

> These concepts share many of the same advantages but also suffer from many of the same problems. For example, a carbon tax could operate with exemptions for a given industry or company in much the same way that credits are given under a cap-and-trade system of taxation. These methods could be imposed at

varying stages from initial production of the energy source to the point of use. In either case, ease of administration argues for imposition at the upstream end.

There are also concerns about the system being gamed. As Tom Friedman cautions, "Cap-and-trade will be managed by Wall Street. If you liked credit-default swaps, you're going to love carbon-offset swaps."

Countering these general perceived advantages for a carbon tax is the need to harmonize our carbon pricing policies with those of other leading industrial nations, who have generally adopted a cap-and-trade system (in large part, skeptics argue that this has happened precisely because a cap-and-trade system allows more opportunities for rent capture [that is, illicit profit-seeking by corrupt politicians and bureaucrats] and illusory carbon reductions, which are, of course, always easier to make than real ones). Many analysts perceive that using a carbon tax would make it much more difficult for the United States to enter into an emissions trading scheme with other areas of the globe, resulting in a loss of economic efficiency for the entire enterprise. Further, if other jurisdictions do not adopt some sort of carbon pricing, the United States will be at a competitive disadvantage. Also, in order to diminish disruption to industry, some analysts have suggested that any pricing on carbon must be phased in on a gradual basis, taking into account the evolving costs and benefits in such a scheme.

Further, some Task Force members felt that using government revenues from a carbon cap or carbon tax to fund unrelated programs confused the issue. Therefore, any revenues raised from such a tax should be offset so the system is revenue neutral. Generally speaking, however, legislative proposals for cap-and-trade or carbon taxes have lacked this component of revenue neutrality and themselves can be attacked as taking private funds out of the economy.

To explore some of these issues further, the Task Force invited Larry Goulder, the Shuzo Nishihara Professor of Environmental and Resource Economics at Stanford and a Task Force member, to make a presentation on this subject during Hoover's energy conference. Moderating was Roger Noll, professor of economics emeritus at Stanford University and a senior fellow at the Stanford Institute for Economic Policy Research. Noll helped design and implement one of the first versions of a cap-and-trade policy. The discussant was Terry Dinan, the senior adviser on climate issues at the Congressional Budget Office, who has been a longtime staff economist at the Environmental Protection Agency and who was speaking in a personal capacity.

Proceedings

In his approach to the subject, Goulder built on many of the Task Force's earlier conclusions but particularly stressed the importance of "second-best solutions" in the policy realm, noting that often the best solutions from an academic perspective are not politically feasible. As an example, he cited the California commission that he and his Energy Task Force colleague Jim Sweeney had recently served on and noted that he and Sweeney had joined in a commission recommendation on the implementation of a carbon cap-and-trade (which Sweeney personally opposes) on the grounds that, if California is going to do a cap-and-trade policy, it should do the best version possible.

He also noted the appropriateness of putting the carbon pricing problem in a global context.

China uses more coal than the United States, India, and Japan combined. Even if China were to sign onto a strong or stronger than Copenhagen agreement to reduce greenhouse gas emissions, it is very unclear that cap-and-trade or something similar that puts a price on carbon will get us the game-changing technologies that we need in order to have very sharp reductions in greenhouse gas emissions.

Furthermore, as Goulder argued, there is a role for both a technology push and emissions pricing policies. Inventors do not capture the full value of their inventions and thus are not sufficiently motivated to invent. Such incentives could be created through either a subsidy to R&D or through changes in patent laws.

Goulder argued that there are many misleading arguments made about the varying merits of carbon tax versus cap-and-trade. He said that we should promote not what he called "simple cap-and-trade" but a "hybrid cap-and-trade" that combines the best features of cap-and-trade and carbon tax. He called price volatility the soft underbelly of simple cap-and-trade.

Such a cap should have an upper "safety valve" price at which carbon emitters could purchase unlimited numbers of permits, giving emitters some comfort and some ability to price their carbon emissions risk more accurately. Goulder argued the equivalence of the cap-and-trade and carbon tax systems. In one scenario you are setting the price, which will ultimately determine the quantity of emissions—and on the other you are setting the quantity, which will determine the price of those emissions. Critics would note, however, that one principal difference between the policies is that with cap-and-trade, you get a guaranteed amount of emissions at an uncertain price, while with a carbon tax, the amount of emissions could theoretically have no limit at all, provided people were willing to pay the price of the tax.

Dinan agreed with Goulder that the potential differences in implementation between carbon tax and cap-and-trade had been significantly overstated, but she added that industry preferred cap-and-trade because of the potential value of free allowances it could obtain. Dinan argued that carbon tax was inherently more efficient than cap-and-trade because carbon was a stock pollutant rather than a flow pollutant (that is a pollutant whose damage depends on the aggregate amount emitted rather than the amount emitted at any one particular time) and that taxes work better on stock pollutants. Having a fixed additional price for a stock pollutant (as is typical with a carbon tax) is usually more efficient than having a highly variable price, as is possible with cap-and-trade (in which the price can vary dramatically depending on how many permits are available at any given time).

Another advantage of a tax over a cap is that, if economists have a reasonable sense of the potential range of monetary damage, they can make sure that the tax falls within that range. This is not possible to do with a cap-and-trade system.

For this reason, Dinan argued against the notion of harmonizing our policies and our carbon trading network with those of other countries, saying that it would potentially allow weak credits from countries with poor enforcement mechanisms to crowd out strong credits to countries with better enforcement mechanisms. For this reason, Dinan added, pure cap-and-trade is passé.

> Almost no one is talking about a pure cap-and-trade program any more. Economists have started thinking about how we can add

bells and whistles to cap-and-trade programs to help them capture some of the desirable efficiency characteristics of a tax. That
has been an interesting development, but it has also made com-
paring these policies much more difficult.

Roger Noll added that in his experience in designing a cap-and-
trade program a central appeal of this approach was that it was
less subject to political meddling over longtime horizons.

> Politicians can always say they want to cut taxes, but it is harder
> to "cut" cap-and-trade and the special interests that get extra
> allowances can just trade them away.

He also agreed that innovation was a critically important piece
and that we systematically underinvested in innovation.

Goulder noted that critics of cap-and-trade, such as climatol-
ogist Jim Hansen, have referred to it as something that "merely
allows polluters and Wall Street traders to fleece the public out
of billions of dollars." But Goulder disputed this assertion. He
noted that Hansen's scenario only applied, if at all, in a situation
in which vast numbers of permits were given away to emitters.
By ensuring that all permits were instead auctioned, as he and
Sweeney have recommended, this problem would go away. He
noted that previous caps have been poorly designed and that
even the politically unviable Waxman-Markey climate bill currently before Congress had hugely excessive subsidies for major
polluters (over 80 percent more than necessary according to
Goulder's research). He said that California appeared to be
bucking this trend toward excess giveaways of permits.

Goulder stressed the importance of an upstream tax for
administrative ease, to avoid charging all of the hundreds of
thousands of small-scale carbon emitters. An upstream tax
would limit the taxation to only a few hundred entities. He

argued that a cap-and-trade or carbon tax could be harmonized with other international systems, though he acknowledged that doing this would have some effect under WTO rules.

> It is easier to harmonize a new federal carbon cap-and-trade system with existing cap-and-trade systems than to try to harmonize a domestic carbon tax with those systems.

Goulder noted that the price volatility potentially presents huge problems without a price cap. California's "RECLAIM" clean air program saw the price of its permits go up by more than an order of magnitude in one year. Others have noted that very volatile prices are more likely to bring speculators into the market, which may have deleterious effects.

Dinan responded that she was not as sure that volatility was necessarily a major problem for the market as she believed it could be solved with emissions banking for credits (in RECLAIM, credits could not be banked). She also argued that players in the private market may enter into long-term carbon credit contracts to reduce their volatility, as they have done in the natural gas market.

On the issue of market gaming, Goulder was skeptical that things were as bad as they potentially appeared.

> My initial thinking about this is that the potential [for market gaming] is not so clear. If you think of the direct gaming, that is, in terms of holders of allowances trying to reduce the supply or somehow hoard the supply in order to affect the prices, it seems that the potential for that is going to be relatively small because there is going to be a larger number of players and a very big market, a thick market. Now you might think that there is still a possibility for shenanigans in the secondary market or the market

of speculators. But is there really a market failure there? Some would say that speculators can actually help markets work better. So I think that remains an open issue.

Goulder said that researchers such as Robert Stavins at Harvard have argued that, while in a carbon tax system various industries will try to exempt themselves, thus reducing its efficiency, in a cap-and-trade system people will only try to go for more allowances, which will have less effect on efficiency.

Finally Goulder touched on the issue of gasoline taxes as an alternative to carbon taxes and claimed that these conceivably could be justified on the grounds of externalities, such as local pollution and congestion, but that gas taxes should not be used as a substitute for a carbon tax or cap-and-trade. Goulder alluded to research suggesting that local pollution externalities alone would call for a roughly fifty cent gasoline tax increase above the current tax increases.

Recommendations

◊ A pure cap-and-trade system is a poor idea, and we should work to avoid this solution in favor of some form of a carbon tax or a cap-and-trade system with a safety valve price. But while cap-and-trade is not the ideal system, even this is preferable to inaction.

◊ The cap should have a price floor as well as a price ceiling in order to avoid artificially skewing prices downward. However, there is a possibility that such ceilings would leave people open to price manipulation, a subject which needs more empirical study.

⬥ Offsets in either a cap-and-trade or carbon-tax market need to be looked at with great skepticism. There is a high potential for abuse of a system that is too generous with offsets.

⬥ Whatever resources are collected by a cap-and-trade tax or a carbon tax should be refunded to the general public. A revenue-neutral system will then not be a tax drag on the economy.

SESSION 6

A Sustained Research and Development Policy

*"I believe that we have three Sputniks for our generation:
there is energy security, greenhouse gas emissions
and climate change, and, of course, the
U.S. technological lead."*

—ARUN MAJUMDAR

Overview

RESEARCH, DEVELOPMENT, AND DEPLOYMENT of new energy technologies will be at the heart of any solution to the environment-energy conundrum. Experience dating back to the Montreal Protocol, which eliminated the usage of ozone-depleting chemicals and is widely viewed as by far the most successful global environmental treaty, shows that the development of new technologies (in the Montreal Protocol's case, refrigerants that do not deplete the ozone layer) is the key to making environmental progress, even if one accepts a framework in which international negotiations are at the center of the effort.

If you think that domestic policies will rule the day, the development of technologies is even more important. Without plausible cost-competitive alternatives to existing energy technologies, people are extremely unlikely to adopt new ones.

The United States has traditionally put very little money into energy R&D. Expenditures in 2008 were well below what they were even in the late 1970s, when the oil crisis pushed the government into an aggressive innovation posture, one that saw the first serious deployments of wind and solar energy.

With the most recent energy price spikes, as well as concerns about energy security, interest in alternative energy solutions has soared, as has the government's involvement.

In particular there is great interest in how the government interacts with the private sector to spur energy innovation, especially in gaps between the basic research funded by government and the traditional venture capital model.

To discuss the direction of this involvement, the Energy Task Force assembled a panel of experts. Sid Drell, noted physicist, a board member of the group that supervises National Labs at Livermore and Los Alamos, and a recipient of the Department of Energy's Enrico Fermi Award, moderated. The presenter was Arun Majumdar, recently appointed director of ARPA-E (Advanced Research Projects Agency-Energy, a new government agency encouraging research and development of advanced energy technologies). ARPA-E is modeled after DARPA (Defense Advanced Research Projects Agency, known for, among other things, developing the Internet). Prior to his service at ARPA-E he was deputy director at Lawrence Berkeley National Lab where he was also director of the energy and environmental technologies division. He is also a professor of mechanical engineering at UC Berkeley. The respondent was Mike Goguen, a partner at Sequoia Capital, one of the world's leading venture capital firms, where he focuses on "cleantech" (energy technology) investments. Prior to Sequoia, he held a variety of engineering and management roles at a number of major technology companies.

Panelists agreed that existing venture capital models were not adequate for capital-intensive energy development and that groups such as ARPA-E could provide valuable "bridge" financing for technologies not yet ready for commercial investment but past the basic research stage. They also agreed that U.S. energy technology funding at the governmental level had lagged badly. There was some discussion and contention among Task Force members about whether this funding lag was due primarily to structural or political factors.

Proceedings

Sid Drell began by sketching an overall vision for energy technology development.

> There is no lack of vision of the goals we aspire to. We know what we want R&D to accomplish for us: developing technologies and systems that meet our energy needs. The question should be: How to get there?

Arun Majumdar compared the current need for an energy revolution with the explosion in U.S. government-backed scientific research that began after the Soviets launched the Sputnik satellite in the 1950s.

> I believe that we have three Sputniks for our generation: there is energy security, greenhouse gas emissions and climate change, and, of course, the U.S. technological lead.

He said that the time frame for such innovations needed to be fast.

> I think what we really need today is a system to develop and encourage the brightest minds in the energy area so that we can hope to see game-changing innovations happening in a span of ten to twenty years.

Majumdar stressed biofuels, batteries, and photovoltaics as the most promising areas for innovation. He also said that under-appreciated areas like energy efficient buildings offered great promise.

> This is the biggest chunk of the energy use in the United States. Seventy-two percent of the electricity goes into buildings. The grid is essentially there because of buildings.
>
> Let us hypothesize that energy consumption was today 80 percent less in new buildings and 50 percent less in the old buildings. It would mean that we would essentially eliminate the need for half the coal-fired power plants in this country and if the remaining need were balanced out with nuclear, hydro, and others, you would have no carbon emissions from electricity.

But he noted that there are several technological impediments to making those improvements.

> In the building sector we need new technologies for lighting, heating, cooling, real-time measurements, system integration and human interfaces, measurement-based energy and indoor-environment performance standards, financial incentives and disincentives based on actual measurement—essentially architecture, engineering, business, public policy all combined. We do not have that. If you can make a building with energy consumption decreased by 50–80 percent and have a payback period of three

years or two years, it is a no-brainer. The question is how do you get there?

He said other primary challenges that were a focus of ARPA-E included lowering battery costs from $1000 per kWh to $250 per kWh and increasing the potential for grid-level electricity storage, which is almost nonexistent in today's electricity grid.

> We cannot store electricity in our infrastructure. Can we develop grid-level storage at less than a hundred dollars per kilowatt hour? Solar energy utilization that is less expensive than fossil fuels? Carbon capture and utilization at a cost which is less than its price? If we can do that someone will make money out of it, but we cannot do that today.

Mike Goguen then stepped in to speak to the issue of technological innovation from the venture capitalist's perspective, stressing that the most important role government could play in innovation policies was helping to build genuinely sustainable industries.

> The trick really is how do we use national policy, how do we use something like ARPA-E so that it not only acts as a catalyst but also gets the motivations aligned so that people are building real companies, not ones based on artificiality? A market that only makes sense with a permanent subsidy is artificial. I think it has probably been a good thing that there have been international subsidies to stimulate solar market development, because now you see intense competition. This will drive the costs lower and lower. Now we are nearing a point where the companies can stand on their own.

Goguen praised the idea behind ARPA-E.

> The ARPA-E program comes very close to the bull's-eye, for venture capital at least. There are a lot of technology examples—

potentially great companies, but they are a little earlier in the development process than we are used to. There is more risk than in the typical IT investment. What you really need in those cases is that little bit of extra help, so the three, four, five million dollars from the government will help if they choose wisely.

Goguen stressed that government money would be best given to start-ups, not established players, but that there needed to be equal wariness of not giving money to excessively academic entities.

I would be a little leery of giving money to giant companies that have huge R&D budgets already. At the other extreme, if it is pure research in a pure university with pure academics that do not show any inclination to ever build a company, I assume there are other funding vehicles for that. I would focus on these wonderful technology-oriented investment opportunities, perhaps coming out of the university but with very entrepreneurial professors behind them who want to start a company. These are typically a little early in the game for VCs but with the help of ARPA-E's funding, the gap could be bridged.

Sid Drell mentioned the legendary Bell Labs as a model for energy innovation here.

I am reminded when I think about this problem of the enormous success of Bell Labs for several decades following World War II, where with the enlightened leadership of Mervin Kelly the centrality of free thinking, creativity, taking risks was well understood. All this took place within a program direction dedicated to improving communications for AT&T.

Andy Karsner, himself a former assistant secretary of energy, said that much of the problem lay in the DOE's culture as well as in the very different nature of energy technologies, as compared to traditional venture capital technologies.

> Hopefully you can change DOE, because DOE is inadequate for its mission on energy security. How do we move things through the continuum from basic research into business plans and commercial ventures that scale, with capital formation? That is the paradigm that we have talked about. But the analogy that we have for this in Silicon Valley is software and IT and telecom: technologies other than energy. The dilemma that we have is that software and IT really scales, relative to the energy industry, at no cost of distribution and no cost in scaling. But with energy no matter what energy source you are talking about you are talking about a capital-intensive commodity trading sector. Ultimately you are into a commodity business that has no distribution channel like FedEx or the Internet. We are talking ten-year time frames to make that translation from technology into commodities. So that is our dilemma.

Majumdar agreed with Karsner that a new funding model was needed.

> ARPA-E has been called the venture capital center of DOE. That is a little misleading. We are looking at the return for the nation and that is not just in dollars. In some areas the venture capital model is perfectly fine. But a large demonstration project needs a lot of capital and that may not be the venture capital model. How do we get demonstration projects, which have been in the past only for performance, also to have a cost metric?

Majumdar was also asked about where basic research would fit into the equation, since basic research did not seem to be part of ARPA-E's mandate. Majumdar responded that moving earlier in the research cycle was a goal of ARPA-E.

ARPA-E's mandate is to take technologies and make them business ready, whether it is from a university or a national lab or a small business. If the technology is in an early stage and is not yet business ready, we are mandated to reduce the technology risk and help to get it market ready. That said, we could intervene a little earlier in the process. ARPA-E is being reauthorized right now. We are trying to see whether we can provide the tools to help science acquire the knowledge which will eventually help us. That is something that we will certainly look at.

Lucy Shapiro related her own experience with the vital nature of "bridge" funding for laboratory technologies.

In 1999 we had an idea in our laboratory. I work on the genetic circuitry of the simple bacterial cell. We said, "Look at this. We have a circuit. We have a node in the circuit. That is going to provide a new target for antibiotics, different from what everybody else is doing." We really need this, yet this is very basic research and it is basic research that is not going to be funded by the NIH because we really had not a lot to back it up. It was an idea. We went to DARPA and DARPA said, "The chance of this working is 10 percent? 5 percent? We are going to fund you." And they funded us. We got something like a million and a half dollars. I teamed up with a chemist and we made a whole new class of boron-based compounds that ultimately developed into Anacor, a company in Silicon Valley, and now we have new antibiotics, new antifungals. If we had not gotten that money from DARPA, it never would have happened. There is nobody right now in ARPA-E and in the DOE who is funding very, very basic research.

Burt Richter noted that the United States has a long history of throwing away technologies for which it has developed basic research.

We developed nuclear reactors here. We do not do that anymore. Computer memory. Here. We do not do that anymore. People forget that if you are talking about wind turbines the big advance was here. We threw that away. That is now in Denmark. Now you can go down that whole list.

Goguen echoed Richter's concern and said much of the problem was structural, rather than political.

Sequoia has close to twenty-five companies in this sector. Almost half are profitable already, but that half is not in the United States. It is our India and China cleantech or energy companies that happen to be the profitable ones. None of the U.S. ones are yet. So far, it is very difficult to beat the cost structures, especially on the manufacturing side, and a lot of these things are manufacturing intensive. Market forces are steering us in a direction whereby even if the innovations are coming out of the United States, they will be manufactured elsewhere.

Paul Berg noted that energy innovation needed to follow the basic research model found in other sectors of government.

We have to think about knowledge generation as a spectrum. The National Institutes of Health invest heavily in understanding basic biological processes. The National Science Foundation funds that kind of very fundamental untargeted research. So we have a continuum, from very fundamental untargeted research through applications research. The industrial sector and venture capital are rarely interested in the early phases. So that is why we have to keep the National Institutes of Health and its counterparts in the physical sciences very healthy. Otherwise we will use up much of what we know and the basic knowledge to fuel the next breakthrough will be lacking.

To Majumdar, the problem transcended partisan boundaries, and the energy research deficit went back more than twenty-five years.

> If you look back at the last two and a half decades you can see that the focus on energy was really lost. Adding to the base of people looking at energy and studying it in depth was lost.

Task Force chair George Shultz said problems of allocating the funding of research money had been long-standing in government.

> When I was director of the budget in the 1970s, I could see that even research was skewed by politics. How do you get some money that gives you the right orientation? There was a science advisory board of some sort, so I got them convened for a meeting and all they did was argue about "more money should go to me" and so on. I listened to this for an hour and a half and decided I was going to get no help from them. So you really had to make a deal with the people running places like DARPA and with the secretary of defense. They were going to seek appropriations in such a way that they have room to maneuver. Then you count on the fact that you have somebody in charge that has the courage and the conviction to use that ambiguity constructively.

Task Force member Tom Stephenson said that treating energy like another technology would fall short of the necessary solution.

> Because of the amount of money required to develop some of the basic technologies that relate to energy, we may well have a gap. The issue is where is the missing piece of the puzzle? Where is the funding going to come from? The disciplines of the venture capital community are really important, because venture capital-

ists will figure out, when something is at a certain stage, whether or not it really does have the ability to make money over the long term. But there will be a piece where the venture capital community is not going to be ready to fund it, and yet it is not clear that this piece really meets the definition of basic research. So I do think we have a different situation here in the energy world than we do in some other areas of technology.

Robert Edwards noted that we need to make a clean distinction between the world of venture capital that Silicon Valley is comfortable with and the emerging and new world of energy innovation.

There are big differences between the high-tech world that we are comfortable with here in Silicon Valley and the old style energy world that we are dealing with. What policy is going to be in place over the long term to deal with the problem of a game-changing technology that never sees the light of day in a utility because they will be slow to change their acquisition protocols? A breakthrough in cellulosic ethanol can only reach the light-duty vehicle market through major investments in infrastructure. The question is how do we think about the gap between energy innovation and commercialization?

Goguen agreed that utility adoption would be a key to reform and said that progress was being made in this area.

In the past five to six years the utilities looked at new technologies and finally thought, "Wait a minute, this actually makes sense for us. This actually saves us money." They started to purchase smart-grid software, smart-grid hardware in 2008, early 2009. At that point some well-intended incentive was introduced to help the utilities move to smart grids faster. Then the industry ground to a sudden halt. The reason was obvious. The utilities said, "Wait a minute, is there going to be a program that might give this to us free?" Venture-backed opportunities are the ones where we strive to find what is going to make sense for this big sleepy industry without too much artificiality.

Sid Drell closed with an observation that the problems of technology innovation (and even clean-energy innovation) had much deeper roots in history than just the last few decades.

President Lincoln created the National Academy during the Civil War in 1863. He created the Department of Agriculture. When he created the land grant universities, they had big departments of agriculture because he was extremely interested in future developments in that area. In fact, he spoke about the importance of advancing the sciences of soil and mechanization. He commented on this enormous source of energy out there, the winds blowing over the plains, but he did not know what to do about it. He noted that it had been talked about as long ago as Isaiah and they still had only been able to use it to push boats with sails.

Recommendations

A basic component of American national policy must be to establish and maintain a strong research and development program that advances the goal of achieving energy efficiency and independence with technologies that are safe and environmentally friendly. What is needed is: adequate, steady support for a broad scientific and technical base for the program that would encourage transformative scientific discoveries and directed programmatic advances. And specifically:

⬧ A balanced program based on these principles will attract the top quality scientists and engineers that are critical for success.

⬧ To the greatest degree possible, not to pick technology winners at the Federal Government level.

⬧ For the Federal Government to focus intensively on creating an environment to nurture a broad suite of technologies, paying particular attention to the gap between basic research and projects that are mature enough to receive venture funding.

SESSION 7

*Emerging International
Energy Relationships*

*"My read of the history of international efforts to deal with
energy and environmental issues is that, pretty much,
success or failure follows innovation. When technologies
are available at a reasonable cost and good performance,
everything that is hard to do in international cooperation
gets much easier."*

—DAVID VICTOR

Overview

OUR GREATEST OPPORTUNITIES to affect energy policy take
place at the state, local, and national levels, but the issues of
energy economics, security, and climate policy are necessarily
global in nature. The energy policies of emerging powers such
as China and India, as well those of oil-rich states such as Saudi
Arabia, have major effects on the United States energy policy.

The United States and Europe can adopt the most aggressive
possible targets and cutting edge emissions-reduction technology—all of which will make little difference if India, China, and

other developing nations generate emissions of carbon as they develop their economies.

Yet, for all of the centrality of international energy issues, our international institutions for energy cooperation have not kept up with the new challenges. The International Energy Agency (IEA), formed in the wake of the 1973 oil crisis, has its strengths, but China and India are not even members.

The virtual collapse of climate talks at Copenhagen and the inadequacy of the Kyoto regime underscore the weakness of broad-based global efforts to contain climate change and to harmonize climate imperatives with global energy needs.

To examine these difficult problems, the Energy Task Force assembled a panel at its conference to examine international energy relationships and how we could improve them.

Moderating and participating in the panel was David Victor, a Task Force member, formerly director of the Program on Energy and Sustainable Development at Stanford and now professor at the School of International Relations and Pacific Studies at the University of California, San Diego. Victor is one of the world's leading scholars of international energy relationships and governance. Joining Victor on the panel were Michael Wara, an assistant professor at Stanford Law School and a leading expert in international climate negotiation, and Charles Ebinger, director of the Energy Security initiative and senior fellow at the Brookings Institution, who has advised more than fifty governments around the world on energy policy issues in more than thirty-five years in the energy field.

The discussion and debate ranged over a diverse set of issues including climate change, oil and natural gas policy, energy security, global energy markets, innovation policy, and carbon markets. There was wide agreement that the current mode of addressing climate change was broken and that American promises to act on climate issues were not seen as credible. Panelists and other participants also generally agreed that a single carbon market and carbon price on a global basis was neither necessary nor even feasible. In general, there was great suspicion of what one panelist called "hyper-multilateralism"—and an agreement that smaller groups of influential nations acting in concert might be able to make more effective energy and climate policy. While such a structure seemed to finally emerge informally at Copenhagen, the dominance of irrelevant players in the public proceedings served as an unwelcome distraction for those nations committed to doing something serious in the climate policy area.

There were varying views on the ability of the United States to drive global energy innovation, specifically with regard to the possibility of doing so rapidly enough to decrease our near-term oil dependence. Some felt that such innovation was possible, while others felt that a short-to-medium-term attempt to remove the petroleum basis from our economy was a fool's errand. However, there was general agreement among both panelists and other participants that successful innovation policy to develop and deploy new energy technologies should be at the heart of our international energy engagement, in contrast to large multilateral agreements that focus on pledges of possible reductions in global carbon output.

Proceedings

David Victor began the discussion by pointing out that our achieving international goals on climate change and energy security were necessarily dependent on having national goals on these subjects that were credible. Absent credible domestic policies, few international actors were likely to engage meaningfully with the United States. He also noted that, while many task forces on energy have produced strategies for an integrated energy policy, such goals are totally unrealistic for a country with energy decision making as fragmented as it is in the United States.

As Victor noted:

> One of the problems we have as a country in dealing with the international dimensions of this issue is the lack of credibility in the promises that our diplomats bring to international negotiations. We have seen this most recently in Copenhagen. We sent the president to negotiate a deal where we were not even clear that we could deliver on the basic and modest things that the president was promising to the rest of the world, let alone these wild things like providing a hundred billion dollars annually of new money by 2020.

Ebinger agreed with Victor's criticisms of Copenhagen.

> Copenhagen by any standard was a disaster. I think it was an embarrassment to the United Nations at the most basic level.

Ebinger noted that among other problems, the conference was so disorganized that Assistant Secretary of Energy David Sandalow, one of the leading U.S. negotiators, was shut out of negotiations for a time because of a credentialing problem. He also echoed Victor's critique that promises, like Obama's pledge to help deliver $100 billion annually by 2020, were empty.

> I just don't see in the current climate where there's any political will to raise that kind of money.

Task Force member Andy Karsner echoed Ebinger's sentiments and offered a potential future vision for a more productive set of international talks.

> It is important that we not talk only about who you are convening but also about the rules by which the diplomacy takes place. You cannot have credibility if you have no expertise at the table—with environmental regulators talking past one another and with NGOs sort of cheering them on. But what major nations negotiating can give us is representatives of the heads of state plus three: finance, technology and trade. It can give us a schedule and a frequency for the principal representatives of the heads of state to meet. The administration may have learned that they need to get back on that track behind closed doors, closed to the media, too, if they actually want a globally inclusive accord that can feed into the UN process.

The panelists also expressed their views on international energy markets. Ebinger urged the United States to avoid the temptations of energy autarky.

> I for one do not believe we should or can totally move away from petroleum.

And he added:

> I do not believe that OPEC is an enemy. They are certainly dictatorships. They certainly have their own international agenda, but I think to retreat into some kind of energy autarky is not only foolhardy, but in any reasonable time horizon we have no other alternative for our transportation sector. We have today 246 million vehicles on the road. You show me when we are going to have 5, 10 million electric cars.

Jim Woolsey dissented from Ebinger's skepticism on electric vehicles, pointing out that intelligent innovation policies such as Japan's can rapidly increase fleet vehicle turnover and lead to more rapid adoption of new technologies. He also stressed that he believed oil merely needed to have its role as a strategic commodity in transportation eliminated, not that its use should be eliminated altogether. Vehicles that could run on electricity, biofuels, or other alternatives to gasoline, could accomplish this.

Karsner added an additional perspective, saying that, while he did not dispute factually that moving from oil as a transport fuel in the near term was difficult, there was, nonetheless, a large strategic imperative for the United States' attempting to do so.

With respect to the international dimensions of energy innovation policy, Victor added that he viewed innovation as a key element of an engaged U.S. global energy strategy. He mentioned DARPA and the new ARPA-E as models for developing this capability and said that researchers in the United States needed to be much more engaged at exactly where the gaps in the current innovation pipeline are.

Victor argued that the ability to innovate successfully to reduce energy costs was critical to developing international energy partnerships, which is why he viewed the subject as such an important piece of the puzzle.

> My read of the history of international efforts to deal with energy and environmental issues is that, pretty much, success or failure follows innovation. When technologies are available at a reasonable cost and good performance, everything that is hard to do in international cooperation gets much easier. For example, if you have reluctant countries who do not want to do something, it is easier to buy them off if it is not so expensive. Questions of defectors, monitoring, and enforcement—all perennial troubles in

international law—are easier to manage in a world where the overall costs are lower.

Ebinger agreed that both technological innovation and implementing flexibility were important and also stressed that it was vital that U.S. international engagement not forget the huge number of global poor who lack access to commercial energy.

> We seemed to have forgotten the 1.6 billion people in the world who have no electricity and probably another 500 million people with electricity who may have one or two light bulbs and perhaps a fan. As we look towards a global climate regime, we cannot tell these people that they cannot increase their energy consumption and must remain at a substandard level of living because if we do, we will have more failed states, more political crises, more international terrorism, and that cannot and must not be what we do as leaders of the world.

He noted that particularly in India and China, support for coal was seen as absolutely critical in domestic politics. Given the criticality of coal usage in the domestic economies of the two biggest developing countries, he identified carbon capture and storage (CCS) from coal-fired power plants as the critical energy technology to innovate.

> But coal around the world is a major provider of jobs. So finally I think if I had to make one recommendation, I would say we must push forward with CCS technology. If we want these other countries to curtail the way they currently burn coal, we have to be a leader in the technology. I would urge the president and the rest of his administration to put together, as they already are trying to, some task forces involving Indians, Chinese, and other major coal producers, where they come together, work together, and prove that CCS is both technically and commercially viable.

Victor, while agreeing about the centrality of coal, dissented from this broader recommendation, arguing that, rather than engaging in pie-in-the sky technologies such as CCS, there was more opportunity to do basic technological improvements on power plant efficiency and that this would have a bigger reward. Victor agreed that it was vitally important from a development perspective to bring commercial energy to those now lacking it and that the actual impact of this on carbon emissions would be negligible (about a 1 percent increase in global emissions, making reasonable assumptions about energy usage from these low-income families).

In the area of international climate negotiations, Victor saw the international consensus moving toward cap-and-trade versus carbon tax, although in a fragmented way.

> Cap-and-trade seems to be easier, politically, because it seems to offer a greater ease in wiring the politics, because if you are a politician with cap-and-trade you get to give away all these emissions credits to your friends for free. Every country is going to go through that process in a different way. The Europeans have different allocation rules from ours. We here in the United States are going to have different allocation rules. We could conceivably have a federal system along with multiple state systems running in parallel.

Victor noted that the fragmentation of global carbon markets was an indication of the seriousness with which some countries were treating the climate problem.

> What we have seen is the creation of many different carbon markets; the more serious countries get about taming global warming, the more carbon markets become fragmented. It is identical to the question of why we do not have a single global currency, because we have lots of different national interests and institutions.

Wara agreed with Victor about the futility of a single global carbon market and carbon price.

> I think that the global carbon market and the global price for carbon is probably a blind alley that we should be wary about expending too much political capital on and about letting it distract our attention from more critical issues.

He also argued that the most useful climate negotiations would eventually take place between a few major emitters, with the UN process increasingly becoming a sideshow. Ebinger agreed with this assessment.

Victor said he believed many of the problems with our current energy and climate negotiations were a function of what he called "hyper-multilateralism."

> We are in the middle of a shift back away from hyper-multilateralism because multilateral systems work well in some settings, but they have a huge cost, a cost that was on display every day in Copenhagen, which is that they diffuse benefits and they diffuse responsibility. Serious governance is hard to craft when benefits and responsibilities are diffused. Instead, the odds of success in crafting a durable climate agreement that actually reduces emissions are much higher if benefits and responsibilities are concentrated.

Wara agreed with Victor that much current multilateral activity was really just disguised unilateralism. Wara noted that agreements to reduce carbon from China and India were heavily conditioned by their interests in natural gas, oil, and energy security, with the climate piece only at the tail of such considerations.

> If you take this entire picture together, it starts to look like international climate policy may be much more about what countries are willing to do domestically in terms of their energy policy

commitments than what we can as an international community bind ourselves to that will move the ball forward.

Task Force member Condoleezza Rice agreed with this assessment.

I think that is actually the most likely outcome and it is because climate policy cuts across two generally higher priorities for national governments: economic policy and energy policy, which are linked.

In response to a question from Rice about how the panel would suggest approaching future climate negotiations, Wara offered advice to the administration.

The administration needs to identify areas where the interests of the key developing countries align with positive climate outcomes and then fund that. Part of what is missing now is a developed-world commitment to negotiate on and identify things that we know how to do now, that can be implemented on the ground in developing countries, would make a difference, and are in the interests of developing countries to do.

Victor suggested that the administration structure its negotiations more along the lines of the WTO accession talks.

In my view, the model is WTO accession talks. What you want countries to do is put on the table the things that they are planning to do with the country. You also want them to put on the table the other things that they would do if other countries did something. This way, you start to break the current problem, which is that everybody only puts on the table what they are willing to do and then they staple it together into a big agreement and they declare a success. You want a dynamic where these commitments become more interdependent.

Rice stressed that clear communication with partners was vital for any administration entering negotiations on international energy and climate issues. She noted on a controversial statement about "addiction to oil" that was put, after careful deliberation, into one of President Bush's State of the Union speeches.

> It was then left to me as secretary of state to call the Canadians and Mexicans to say, "We didn't mean you."

Moving to issues of international cooperation on technology issues, Task Force member Paul Berg raised the issue of geoengineering and expressed concern that too little attention was being paid to this question at a global level.

Wara and Victor both agreed that this was a critical issue, both because of the legal consequences of the potential testing and the question of who would decide when action was actually needed. Wara referred to the entire scenario as "frightening to contemplate." Task Force member Burton Richter expressed skepticism about the wisdom of geoengineering, experiments at this stage of our understanding the consequences, noting that meddling with the atmosphere in this way could open up unknown dangers.

Wara stressed that the administration should place a higher diplomatic priority on encouraging growth of energy governance capacity in emerging economies. He said that U.S. efforts to fund energy governance capacity in places like China through the efforts of groups such as the Natural Resources Defense Council and Lawrence Berkeley National Lab had already paid substantial dividends in terms of Chinese policy implementation (at one recent point, there were fewer people managing energy policy in China than collecting energy statistics in the United States).

Recommendations

- We need to end the phase of hyper-multilateralism in international energy and climate negotiations in favor of bilateral and small-group multilateral engagement.
- Climate negotiations are most likely to be successful in the context of broader energy and trade negotiations, which have greater salience for most countries.
- International energy negotiations should emphasize interdependent commitments, where each country agrees to do a certain set of things, and then to do another set of things if other countries will take on commensurate commitments (World Trade Organization accession talks are a possible model).
- It is probably not desirable to create a global carbon price or market—small local and regional markets will do a better job of providing accountability and reasonable pricing.
- Investing in technological innovation will be absolutely critical for facilitating more useful negotiations on both climate and energy security because negotiators need to be able to see an economically and politically viable transition path before they will abandon old technologies.

APPENDIX 1

WORKING WITH CHINA AND INDIA

Throughout the course of our conference, and particularly in our final session on international energy relationships, it became increasingly clear that while U.S. policymakers will play a vital role in addressing the energy and climate challenges of the coming years, it is not possible to succeed in overcoming these challenges if America acts alone.

Even if the United States chooses the wisest course of action in all of the areas that we discussed, it will mean little if other key countries do not choose to meaningfully engage these problems. This is particularly true with respect to climate policy, as climate change is a problem that, by its very nature, demands global cooperation to address.

China and India, the world's two most populous countries with two of the world's fastest growing economies, are particularly critical countries for the United States to engage in the energy and climate realm. To explore how we might best proceed with this engagement, we commissioned short papers on this subject from Task Force member David Victor and Task Force research manager Jeremy Carl, who have spent years studying the energy economics and politics of these two emerging global giants. Their views, of course, are their own.

These papers are provided as appendices to our conversations about energy, as a reminder that if we are to succeed in our energy and climate goals, we must expand our conversations to include the rest of the world.

WHAT CAN AMERICA DO WITH CHINA?

By David Victor

Serious solutions to the twin problems of energy security and global climate change hinge on the actions of China and the United States, which are the world's largest emitters of carbon dioxide, the main human cause of global warming, and the largest users of oil. Other countries matter, but China and the United States are pivotal. Governments in both countries know this and have thus created an ever-growing array of mechanisms for engagement.

The efforts at engagement so far have not achieved much, with the few real achievements in highly specialized areas that are not readily scaled up to serious and broad interaction on energy and environmental topics. Before fruitful negotiations get under way, we need to explore where and how China and the United States could engage with each other.

Most engagement has been fruitless because both the Chinese and American governments have sought interactions that carry few costs and risks, meaning that what passes for engagement does not reflect the underlying interests and administrative capabilities of the two governments. The result is a large number of dialogues but no real impact on the investments and operations that affect energy security and climate change.

The economic crisis is likely to make engagement even harder as both countries focus on internal problems and, as is typical during hard times, demonize their partners as the cause of trouble. Neither country is well served by its failure to promote serious engagement over energy, security, and pressing environmental issues. Doing better requires initiatives on at least three fronts.

First, abandon the bromides that occupy most discussions of engagement. Such bromides are harmful in that they make the

Chinese skeptical of anything the U.S. government proposes. Credibility and trust are essential yet still in short supply.

For example, many analysts claim that the United States can engage China by transferring to it advanced technology and that China can contribute by lowering its trade barriers. Such efforts, they aver, would help China cut energy consumption and staunch its emissions of greenhouse gases. Chinese firms, however, already have access to most top-tier energy technologies, including renewable power, nuclear power, advanced coal combustion, and efficient end-user devices. Trade barriers are few, and in some areas (such as advanced coal technology or the manufacture of solar cells), China is producing at the world's best standard. (India, by contrast, would gain from fuller trade in energy technologies.) This outcome is hardly surprising; China is a world-class manufacturing nation in many areas, and its expertise extends to many energy technologies. Areas where such technologies are not deployed in China are those in which administration of public policies is poor and industry is fragmented—problems that outsiders, such as the U.S. government or industry, can do little to fix.

Second, recognize that the efforts to engage China over oil provide little if any benefit to the country's core interests and that many are threatening. For China, oil is a strategic commodity (according to the International Energy Agency [IEA], China will depend on imports for 60 percent of its oil by 2030), and sensitivities are high. The United States has spearheaded an effort to enlist China (and India) in the IEA, hoping that doing so would make the operation of Chinese oil markets more transparent and would help integrate China's strategic oil reserves into the global system of reserves. Yet the United States has as yet not devoted much diplomatic effort to overcoming opposition to China's membership by existing IEA members, especially those in Europe who fear a loss of influence. Those nations have blocked changes in the rules needed for China to become a member. The United States also demonizes China's efforts to "go out" to get oil supplies (for example, in Sudan) and to create a navy and system of pipelines that China feels necessary to secure its oil supplies. From the Chinese perspective, engagement over oil security carries huge risks that its current strategies will be undermined and that new Western-oriented strategies (for example, membership in the IEA) will fail. Changing those perceptions will require that the United States be more credible in encouraging China to join market-oriented institutions and tolerating China's need to build capabilities (for example, an effective coast guard) to secure ship-borne oil. Joint U.S.-China exercises in key supply choke points, such as the Strait of Malacca and offshore Somalia, could be useful.

Third, recognize that engagement over climate change has produced little benefit for either the United States or China. The countries are talking but until recently have done little else. Washington has leaned on Beijing to take a more positive stance on climate change; Beijing has responded handsomely in the last two years. Some of China's analysts claim that their country is doing more to control climate warming emissions than any other—a claim that is too bold to be true—but China is certainly headed in that direction. Movement on the issue inside China has come not from an epiphany about the dangers of global warming but from Chinese planners finding many areas, such as energy efficiency, in which local priorities, including energy security and pollution control, align with global needs. Both China and the United States, however, are still struggling to find useful things to do together.

The root cause of the struggle has been the lack of a U.S. policy on controlling emissions. Even as that changes—thanks to more climate-friendly policies on the American coasts and the (albeit slow) efforts to devise a national policy in Washington—there remains little to bring the United States and China together. Yet China is the world's largest emitter of greenhouse gases; no scheme for protecting the climate can be effective or politically sustainable without visible progress in China. This means that the United States must abandon efforts to include trade sanctions as part of U.S. climate legislation;

such measures threaten to damage the one area in which the United States and China have successfully engaged (that is, trade and the World Trade Organization). Politically, such a move will be difficult to advance in Washington: the labor unions and Rust Belt politicians are strong, and supporters of trade sanctions and their votes are key to passage of climate legislation. Finding acceptable climate change proposals will require identifying those areas in which China can make policy changes that align with its underlying interests and reduce emissions. Most offers of engagement, such as the joint development of new power plant technologies, have not been viewed by the Chinese government as credible because of the United States' poor track record in sustaining such promises.

Absent such a constructive alternative, China's major mode of engagement with the climate debate has been through investments (mainly from Europe) under the Kyoto Protocol's Clean Development Mechanism (CDM). A careful look at those investments shows that most do not reduce emissions; until there is an attractive alternative, however, China will continue to view the Kyoto Protocol's CDM as the only carrot for engaging with the outside world on climate change.

Discussions about engagement have drifted from reality in part because they have lost sight of the important connection between international engagement and national policy. Most of the heavy lifting in international affairs is done through national policy because international institutions are weak. For this reason, the two countries might do better to signal tacitly to each other areas for engagement through stronger actions at home. For example, both countries could make more serious efforts to control emissions and to limit the demand for oil; they could also make their domestic markets more open to cross-investments that could, in turn, accelerate the diffusion of technology in both directions. Firms and investors, rather than governments, may prove to be the more consequential actors.

Although the history of engagement efforts is not promising, the signs are hopeful. Energy officials from the Obama administration are spending more time in China listening to the new realities that will force the United States to get more serious. Although China's system for investing and deploying new energy technologies is still flawed, it is a rapidly rising player. That rise gives China options, requiring potential partners, such as the United States, to be more relevant. The most substantive announcements of U.S. international policy during the run-up to the Copenhagen conference on global warming came from joint U.S.-Chinese communiqués, including encouraging news of a fresh round of U.S.-China efforts to cooperate on energy, though the size of the planned effort ($15 million per year) is still too small to be relevant. Also, during the past two years Chinese officials have been changing their tune on global warming, in part because they feared that China would be blamed for the world's inability to reach serious agreements. Today, the spotlight is on Washington's gridlock.

What is at stake here is not just the U.S.-China relationship but the vision of how big, important countries can solve common problems. None of the existing international institutions, such as the IEA, the G-8, or the G-20, seems well organized enough to solve problems such as the world's perennial underinvestment in energy research and development. For China, especially, those institutions do a poor job of representing Chinese interests. The United States and China can fix such problems by finding meaningful ways to cooperate and understand each other. They still have a long way to go.

THE U.S.-INDIA CLIMATE AND ENERGY RELATIONSHIP: DEALING WITH A POWER-STARVED COUNTRY

By Jeremy Carl

"Take the United States of America, which already has vast power resources of other kinds. To have an additional source of power . . . does not mean very much for them. No doubt they can use it, but it is not so indispensable for them as for a power-starved or power-hungry country like India."

—JAWAHARLAL NEHRU, SPEECH TO THE INDIAN PARLIAMENT, MAY 10, 1954

President Obama's decision to host Indian prime minister Manmohan Singh for the first official state visit of his presidency is one of many signs that U.S.-India relations, despite occasional fractiousness, have perhaps never been closer or more geopolitically critical. From mistrustful and occasionally hostile beginnings more than a half century ago during India's years as a leader in the nonaligned movement under Nehru, the U.S-India relationship has blossomed tremendously in recent years. And along with it, the U.S.-India energy relationship has developed rapidly.

The U.S.-India energy relationship has grown because India's global profile has grown. India expects to pass Russia soon as the world's third largest CO_2 emitter behind the United States and China. At the same time the United States' interest in India's energy policy has increased dramatically in recent years as India's economic growth makes it a bigger player on the world stage.

Yet, despite India's growing energy needs, it has only very modest domestic energy resources to utilize. India has an estimated 5.8 billion barrels of oil, a fraction of the 1.26 trillion barrels of worldwide recoverable oil and only a few years worth of domestic consumption. It now consumes 2.8 million barrels of oil daily, up almost 1 million barrels per day in the last decade—a number that promises to explode as Indian consumers begin purchasing more automobiles and other energy-intensive goods. India recently passed Russia to become the fourth largest oil consumer after the United States, China, and Japan. India's natural gas reserves are likewise modest at just 1.1 trillion cubic meters (just 0.6 percent of the world's total), despite some substantial offshore finds in recent years.

Nuclear energy supplies less than 2 percent of India's total energy needs and output actually decreased 13 percent in the last fiscal year, reflecting problems with fuel supply and technical difficulties with their reactors. These difficulties were major drivers for India's pursuit of a nuclear energy agreement with the United States—one that was finally signed in late 2008 after several years of difficult negotiating.

In contrast to its deficits of these other fuels, coal is the one fuel that India has in abundance. Unfortunately, this is also the fuel that is the biggest contributor to the threat of global climate change as well as a damager of local health through particulate emissions. India has 58.6 billion tons of proved coal reserves, accounting for 7 percent of the world's total. Coal makes up between 85 and 95 percent (depending on estimates) of India's indigenous fossil fuel reserves on an energy content basis.

And so Nehru's comment from a half century ago would seem to be borne out today. India is indeed power starved, if the measure used is the fuel needed to power India's rapidly advancing industrialization—especially if that must be done without causing climate change. But if the measure is political power, then India does not seem power starved but ascendant. What follows is a more detailed analysis of the key issues in the U.S.-India energy relationship with respect to climate along with suggestions for how the United States can best engage India on these issues.

In the months leading up to and immediately following Copenhagen, India subtly shifted its stance on climate negotiations. While this is obviously a significant fact in and of itself, it is perhaps more significant for what it reveals about India's drive to enhance its international stature and the importance that U.S. policymakers should attach to India's global-status-anxiety in future energy agreements.

The most prominent face behind India's move has been the charismatic environment minister Jairam Ramesh, a U.S.-educated politician and technocrat whose forceful statements of India's position on climate matters have garnered national and international attention, most notably when he dressed down Secretary of State Hillary Clinton during her 2009 visit concerning India's unwillingness to accept a carbon cap. But while Ramesh has grabbed headlines, at a policymaking level the Indian plan is being spearheaded from the top of the Indian government, in particular by Prime Minister Singh and Congress Party president Sonia Gandhi.

India's new approach reflects both an understanding that India does not want to be seen as an obstacle to a global climate deal and, that India, with its large population of low-income coastal residents and its rainfall-dependent agriculture sector, is substantially vulnerable to climate change.

Instead, India is pursuing what Ramesh refers to as a "per capita plus" approach to climate change, a departure from their previous insistence that India would promise not to have higher per capita emissions than any developed country—a pledge widely considered meaningless over the next thirty or more years because of India's low per capita emissions.

While CO_2 emission caps for India remain off the table, the new framework, which stresses commitments bound into domestic law, offers a potentially useful ground for negotiation—and one that focuses on increasing India's efficiency of energy usage, which India would like to do anyway.

At Copenhagen, India put forward several potentially promising initiatives, including the development of a vehicle-fuel efficiency standard by 2011, generating 20 percent of India's installed power from renewables by 2020 and ensuring that 50 percent of India's new coal-fired power plants will utilize more efficient but more expensive supercritical technology by 2020. India also promised a decline in energy intensity (energy use per unit of GDP) of 20–25 percent by 2020.

This approach gives the United States more room to negotiate with India. The Obama administration would very much like India to be part of any new post-Copenhagen climate deal, as Indian (and Chinese) concessions are a virtual necessity for the United States to clinch a meaningful climate agreement domestically.

The United States should focus on adding teeth to these commitments. First, India is currently opposed to adding black carbon emissions to climate negotiations, but given that black carbon may be India's second largest contributor to climate change, this is not likely sustainable. Second, the United States is unlikely to allow India to not differentiate between energy usage among rich and poor citizens. The United States should be sympathetic to the basic development rights of India's 400 million citizens who do not have access to commercial energy, but there are millions of Indians whose lifestyles and consumption are now at developed country levels. These individuals should not expect to hide behind their countrymen's poverty as a way of shirking their own commitments.

Enforcement will also continue to be an issue: India is right to insist on its sovereignty when developing climate laws, but, given the rudimentary levels at which many Indian laws are enforced, a simple writing of domestic laws without any independent inspection or verification of their efficacy is likely to be a nonstarter in negotiations.

As these negotiations play out, the United States must be careful to engage with India in a way that enhances, rather than detracts from, India's status as an emerging global power.

Looking at the lessons from climate policy, what can the United States learn about exercising leverage in its overall energy relations with India?

First, perceptions matter—India still sees itself as an upstart and is acutely aware of the colonial legacy and slights to its honor. Simply by giving the U.S.-India relationship a high profile (exemplified by the top-level push for the 2008 U.S.-India nuclear partnership agreement), President Bush maintained very high approval ratings in India (according to one poll, the highest he had in any country). Obama, while having gotten off to a rockier start, steadied the ship by inviting Manmohan Singh to be the first foreign head of state invited for a state visit during his administration. The United States' increasing popularity among both India's political class and average citizens helped pave the way for the nuclear deal and made it politically viable for India's leaders to put a controversial natural gas pipeline from Iran to India on the back burner.

Second, the United States has an opportunity for leverage by insisting on doing discrete things, rather than looking for broad policy agreements. Particularly on climate issues, India realistically has limited ability to effectively enforce agreements on greenhouse gas reductions. While the country has made tremendous progress, rule of law in several areas is still limited. Focusing on specific projects and the bilateral relationship (as was done on the nuclear deal, where a deal was worked out bilaterally and the rest of the world brought on board with a *fait accompli*) is often easier than working through a larger forum like the UN, where complicated dynamics come into play and the multiplicity of actors often make reaching agreement difficult.

Third, the United States must use its strategic engagement with India carefully, considering when its strategic objectives in different areas may conflict. In many ways, the complicated entwinement of climate policy with other major U.S.-India energy issues, such as the Iran gas pipeline and U.S-India nuclear agreement, is emblematic of the U.S.-India energy relationship. Everything is connected to everything else, and insisting too decisively on winning any one battle at the negotiating table may jeopardize our overall chances for success. While the United States has often treated each element of the relationship in a piecemeal fashion, a more holistic approach will be necessary if America is to maximize its strategic energy partnership with India in the future.

APPENDIX 2

MEMBERS OF THE
SHULTZ-STEPHENSON TASK FORCE
ON ENERGY POLICY

Stephen D. Bechtel, Jr.

MEMBER OF THE TASK FORCE ON ENERGY POLICY

Stephen D. Bechtel, Jr., is chairman retired and a director of Bechtel Group. He is also chairman emeritus and a director of Fremont Group, LLC. He is also chairman of the S.D. Bechtel, Jr., Foundation and the Stephen Bechtel Fund, the business headquarters of which are in San Francisco. Bechtel has served several industry and community organizations as chairman, including the Business Council, the Conference Board, and the National Academy of Engineering. He also served as vice chairman on the California Council for Science and Technology Task Force to advise Governor Schwarzenegger on improving K–12 science and mathematics education. Bechtel currently serves on the Hoover Task Force on Energy and the MIT Energy Initiative External Advisory Board.

Gary S. Becker

ROSE-MARIE AND JACK R. ANDERSON SENIOR FELLOW

MEMBER OF THE WORKING GROUP ON ECONOMIC POLICY

MEMBER OF THE TASK FORCE ON ENERGY POLICY

Gary S. Becker, who won the Nobel Memorial Prize for Economic Science in 1992, is the Rose-Marie and Jack R. Anderson Senior Fellow at the Hoover Institution and University Professor of Economics and Sociology at the University of Chicago. He is an expert in human capital, economics of the family, and economic analysis of crime, discrimination, and population. His current research focuses on habits and addictions, formation of preferences, human capital, and population growth. He is a featured monthly columnist for *Business Week* magazine and is one of the initial fellows of the Society of Labor Economists. In addition to being a Nobel laureate, Becker is a recipient of the 2007 Presidential Medal of Freedom.

Paul Berg
MEMBER OF THE TASK FORCE ON ENERGY POLICY

Paul Berg is currently the Cahill Professor of Biochemistry emeritus at Stanford University. He was born in New York City and received his undergraduate degree from Pennsylvania State University and a PhD in biochemistry from Case Western Reserve University. He joined the faculty of the Stanford School of Medicine in 1959. Professor Berg has received international recognition for his work on the genetic mechanisms through which cells form proteins. He was awarded the Nobel Prize in Chemistry for developing methods to map the structure and function of DNA and for the development of the recombinant DNA technology. He has received the National Medal of Science and is an elected member of the U.S. National Academy of Sciences, the American Philosophical Society, the French Academy of Science, and the Royal Society (London).

Samuel Bodman
MEMBER OF THE TASK FORCE ON ENERGY POLICY

Samuel Bodman is the former U.S. secretary of energy from 2005 to 2009, having previously served as deputy secretary of the treasury and deputy secretary of commerce.

Bodman is a director of DuPont, Hess Corporation, and AES Corporation. A trustee of the Carnegie Institution and Cornell University, he is a member of the National Academy of Engineering and the American Academy of Arts and Sciences. Bodman chairs the

University of Texas Energy Institute Advisory Board and serves on the International Advisory Council of the King Abdullah University of Science and Technology.

He holds a BS in chemical engineering from Cornell and a ScD from MIT, where he was an associate professor of chemical engineering. He then became president and COO of Fidelity Investments; in 1987, he joined Cabot Corporation, where he was chairman, CEO, and director.

Michael J. Boskin

SENIOR FELLOW
MEMBER OF THE TASK FORCE ON ENERGY POLICY
MEMBER OF THE WORKING GROUP ON ECONOMIC POLICY

Michael J. Boskin is a senior fellow at the Hoover Institution and the T. M. Friedman Professor of Economics at Stanford University. He is also a research associate at the National Bureau of Economic Research, serves on several federal advisory panels, and advises heads of state, finance ministries, and central banks around the world. Among other posts, he served as chairman of the President's Council of Economic Advisers from 1989 to 1993.

John F. Cogan

LEONARD AND SHIRLEY ELY SENIOR FELLOW
MEMBER OF THE WORKING GROUP ON ECONOMIC POLICY
MEMBER OF THE WORKING GROUP ON HEALTH CARE POLICY
MEMBER OF THE TASK FORCE ON ENERGY POLICY

John F. Cogan is the Leonard and Shirley Ely Senior Fellow at the Hoover Institution and a professor in the Public Policy Program at Stanford University. His current research is focused on U.S. budget and fiscal policy, social security, and health care. He has devoted a considerable part of his career to public service. He is a member of

Governor Arnold Schwarzenegger's Council of Economic Advisers and serves on the governor's Public Employee Post-Employment Benefits Commission. He has also served on numerous congressional and presidential advisory commissions. He served as deputy director of the U.S. Office of Management and Budget (OMB) from 1988 to 1989, as associate director for economics and government and subsequently associate director for human resources between 1983 and 1986, and as assistant secretary for policy in the U.S. Department of Labor from 1981 to 1983.

Sidney D. Drell
SENIOR FELLOW
MEMBER OF THE TASK FORCE ON ENERGY POLICY
Sidney D. Drell is a Senior Fellow at the Hoover Institution and professor of theoretical physics (emeritus) at the SLAC National Accelerator Laboratory, Stanford University. He is a member of JASON, a group of academic scientists who consult for the government on issues of national importance, a member of the governing boards of LANS and LLNS, the LLCs that currently manage the Los Alamos and Livermore National Laboratories. He has served as a member of the President's Foreign Intelligence Advisory Board and on a number of advisory bodies to the Congress and Intelligence Community.

James E. Goodby, Executive Director
RESEARCH FELLOW
MEMBER OF THE TASK FORCE ON ENERGY POLICY
James E. Goodby is a research fellow at the Hoover Institution and a senior fellow with the Center for Northeast Asia Policy Studies at the Brookings Institution. He was a Distinguished Service Professor at Carnegie Mellon University from 1989 to 1999 and is now a professor emeritus. Goodby rose to the rank of career minister in

the Senior Foreign Service and was given five presidential appointments to ambassadorial rank. During his Foreign Service career he was involved in the creation of the International Atomic Energy Agency and the negotiation of the limited nuclear test ban treaty, START, in the Conference on Disarmament in Europe, and in cooperative threat reduction (the Nunn-Lugar program). Goodby's most recent book is *At the Borderline of Armageddon: How American Presidents Managed the Atom Bomb;* he coauthored *The Gravest Danger: Nuclear Weapons* (Hoover Institution Press, 2003).

Lawrence H. Goulder
MEMBER OF THE WORKING GROUP ON ENERGY POLICY

Lawrence H. Goulder is a professor and chair of the Department of Economics at Stanford University, where he is also a Kennedy-Grossman Fellow in human biology and a senior fellow at Institute for Economic Policy Research. He is also a research associate and a University Fellow of Resources for the Future at the National Bureau of Economics Research. Goulder, who graduated from Harvard College with an AB in philosophy, obtained a master's degree in musical composition from the Ecole Normale de Musique de Paris, and earned a PhD in economics from Stanford in 1982. He was a faculty member in the Department of Economics at Harvard before returning to Stanford in 1989. Goulder has conducted analyses for several government agencies, environmental organizations, and industry groups.

Kenneth L. Judd
PAUL H. BAUER SENIOR FELLOW
MEMBER OF THE TASK FORCE ON ENERGY POLICY

Kenneth L. Judd is the Paul H. Bauer Senior Fellow at the Hoover Institution. He is an expert in the economies of taxation, imperfect competition, and mathematical economies. His current research focuses on tax policy and antitrust issues, as well as developing computational methods for economic modeling. A fellow of the Econometric Society, he is coeditor of the *Journal of Economic Dynamics and Control*, associate editor of the *Economics Bulletin*, and associate editor of *Computational Economics*.

Alexander A. Karsner
MEMBER OF THE WORKING GROUP ON ENERGY POLICY

Alexander A. Karsner was assistant secretary for energy efficiency and renewable energy from 2005 to 2008. He distinguished himself as a principal architect of and contributor to international climate change deliberations toward achieving a post-2012 global energy framework and as America's top regulator for energy efficiency. He brings twenty years of experience in global energy development and project financing across a wide array of conventional and renewable sources. He served as CEO of the power development and consulting firm Enercorp and both director and senior development manager for Wartsila Diesel. Mr. Karsner is currently on the boards of directors of Argonne National Laboratory, Conservation International, and Applied Materials. He is a Distinguished Fellow at the Council on Competitiveness and a leader of the Energy Future Coalition.

Howard H. Leach
MEMBER OF THE TASK FORCE ON ENERGY POLICY

Howard H. Leach serves as president of Leach Capital, LLC, and Foley Timber & Land Company. Leach was U.S. ambassador to France from 2001 to 2005 and a member of the Board of Regents of the University of California from 1990 to 2001, serving as chairman from 1993 to 1995. Leach graduated from Yale University and attended Stanford Graduate School of Business. He served as an officer in the U.S. Air Force from 1953 through 1955 and has served as director of various companies, including as chairman of Hunter Fan Company and Shippers Development Company. Leach also serves on the boards of the American Friends of Versailles, the American University of Paris, the French-American Foundation, the French Heritage Society, and the Haas Business School at the University of California at Berkeley.

Kevin M. Murphy
MEMBER OF THE TASK FORCE ON ENERGY POLICY

Kevin Murphy is the George J. Stigler Distinguished Service Professor of Economics at the University of Chicago Booth School of Business. He received a BA in economics from the University of California at Los Angeles and a PhD in economics from the University of Chicago, writing his thesis on Specialization and Human Capital. Murphy is the recipient of numerous awards and fellowships, including the John Bates Clark Medal of the American Economic Association, a Sloan Foundation Fellowship and an Earhart Foundation Fellowship. He is a Fellow of the Econometric Society, a Faculty Research Fellow at the National Bureau of Economic Research, a member of the American Academy of Arts & Sciences, and the author of more than 50 published articles. His research has covered a wide range of topics including economic growth, income inequality, valuing medical research, rational addiction, and unemployment.

John Raisian
TAD AND DIANNE TAUBE DIRECTOR
MEMBER OF THE TASK FORCE ON ENERGY POLICY

John Raisian, the Tad and Dianne Taube Director of the Hoover Institution and a senior fellow, is a labor economist whose current interests include the application of economic principles to public policy formation and the appropriate role of government in society. He served as senior economist in the U.S. Bureau of Labor Statistics and as special assistant for economic policy and director of research in the U.S. Department of Labor during the first term of the Reagan administration.

William K. Reilly
MEMBER OF THE TASK FORCE ON ENERGY POLICY
William K. Reilly is founding partner of Aqua International Partners, a private equity fund invested in water and renewable energy companies, and senior advisor to TPG Capital, an international investment partnership. Reilly has served as administrator of the U.S. Environmental Protection Agency, president of the World Wildlife Fund, and president of the Conservation Foundation. Reilly is chairman of the ClimateWorks Foundation, chairman emeritus of the World Wildlife Fund, cochair of the National Commission on Energy Policy, chairman of the Nicholas Institute for Environmental Policy Solutions at Duke University, and a director of the Packard Foundation and the National Geographic Society. He serves on the boards of DuPont, ConocoPhillips, and Royal Caribbean International.

Condoleezza Rice
THOMAS AND BARBARA STEPHENSON SENIOR FELLOW
MEMBER OF THE TASK FORCE ON ENERGY POLICY
Condoleezza Rice is the Thomas and Barbara Stephenson Senior Fellow on Public Policy at the Hoover Institution and professor of political science at Stanford University.

From January 2005 to 2009, she served as the 66th secretary of state of the United States. Before serving as America's chief diplomat, she served as assistant to the president for national security affairs (national security adviser) from January 2001 to 2005.

Burton Richter

MEMBER OF THE TASK FORCE ON ENERGY POLICY

Burton Richter is a Nobel laureate (physics, 1976); the Paul Pigott Professor in the Physical Sciences emeritus, Stanford University; former director, SLAC National Accelerator Center; member, National Academy of Sciences; fellow, American Academy of Arts and Sciences and American Association for the Advancement of Science; and past president, American Physical Society and International Union of Pure and Applied Physics. He is a member of the DOE's Nuclear Energy Advisory Committee, chairing its subcommittee on advanced fuel cycles and is on the Precourt Energy Efficiency Center Advisory Council, Stanford University and a member of the JASON Group and the French Atomic Energy Commission Visiting Group. He chaired the influential 2008 American Physical Society's Energy Efficiency Study.

Henry S. Rowen

SENIOR FELLOW

MEMBER OF THE TASK FORCE ON ENERGY POLICY

Henry S. Rowen, a senior fellow at the Hoover Institution, is a professor of public policy and management emeritus at Stanford University's Graduate School of Business and a member Stanford's Asia/Pacific Research Center.

Lucy Shapiro

MEMBER OF THE TASK FORCE ON ENERGY POLICY

Lucy Shapiro is a professor in the Department of Developmental Biology at Stanford University's School of Medicine, where she holds the Virginia and D. K. Ludwig Chair in Cancer Research; she is also director of the Beckman Center for Molecular and Genetic

Medicine. She is a member of the Board of Advisors of the Pasteur Institute, the Ludwig Institute for Cancer Research, and the Lawrence Berkeley National Labs. She founded the anti-infectives discovery company Anacor Pharmaceuticals and is a member of its board of directors. Professor Shapiro has received multiple honors, including election to the American Academy of Arts and Sciences and the National Academy of Sciences. She was awarded the 2005 Selman A. Waksman Award from the National Academy of Sciences, the Canadian International 2009 Gairdner Award, the 2009 John Scott Award, and the 2010 Abbott Lifetime Achievement Award.

George P. Shultz

THOMAS W. AND SUSAN B. FORD DISTINGUISHED FELLOW
CHAIR, TASK FORCE ON ENERGY POLICY
MEMBER OF THE WORKING GROUP ON ECONOMIC POLICY

George P. Shultz is the Thomas W. and Susan B. Ford Distinguished Fellow at the Hoover Institution. He was sworn in on July 16, 1982, as the sixtieth U.S. secretary of state and served until January 20, 1989. In January 1989, he rejoined Stanford University as the Jack Steele Parker Professor of International Economics at the Graduate School of Business and as a distinguished fellow at the Hoover Institution.

Kiron K. Skinner

W. GLENN CAMPBELL RESEARCH FELLOW
MEMBER OF THE TASK FORCE ON ENERGY POLICY

Kiron K. Skinner is the W. Glenn Campbell Research Fellow at the Hoover Institution at Stanford University. She is also an associate professor of history and political science at Carnegie Mellon University. She specializes in the study of American foreign policy, international relations theory, and international security. Most recently, she edited *Turning Points in Ending the Cold War* and co-authored *Strategy of Campaigning: Lessons from Ronald Reagan and Boris Yeltsin*, both of which were published in 2007.

Abraham D. Sofaer

GEORGE P. SHULTZ SENIOR FELLOW IN FOREIGN POLICY AND
   NATIONAL SECURITY AFFAIRS
MEMBER OF THE TASK FORCE ON ENERGY POLICY

Abraham D. Sofaer, who served as legal adviser to the U.S. Department of State from 1985 to 1990, was appointed the first George P. Shultz Distinguished Scholar and Senior Fellow at the Hoover Institution in 1994.

Thomas F. Stephenson

MEMBER OF THE TASK FORCE ON ENERGY POLICY

Thomas F. Stephenson, who joined Sequoia Capital in 1988, focuses on information technology and health care companies. He is a former U.S. ambassador to the Portuguese Republic and spent twenty-two years with Fidelity Investments. He has been active in the affairs of Harvard University over the years, currently serving as a member of the Board of Overseers and its Executive Committee. He has also been a member of the Executive Committee of the Board of Overseers of the Hoover Institution, the Board of Advisors of the Stanford Institute for Economic Policy Research, the Board of Directors of Conservation International, and the Board of Overseers of the Wilson Center Council and a corporate fund vice chairman of the Kennedy Center. He holds an AB from Harvard, an MBA from Harvard Business School, and a JD from Boston College.

James L. Sweeney
SENIOR FELLOW
MEMBER OF THE TASK FORCE ON ENERGY POLICY

James L. Sweeney is a professor of management science and engineering at Stanford University. He also is a senior fellow at the Stanford Institute for Economic Policy Research and at the Hoover Institution. At Stanford, Sweeney was chairman, Department of Engineering-Economic Systems & Operations Research, 1996–98; chairman, Department of Engineering-Economic Systems, 1991–96; director, Center for Economic Policy Research, 1984–86; chairman, Institute for Energy Studies, 1981–85; and director, Energy Modeling Forum, 1978–84. He recently served on the review panel for the State of California Public Interest Energy Research Program, on the National Research Council's Committee on Benefits of DOE R&D in Energy Efficiency and Fossil Energy, and on the National Research Council's Committee on Effectiveness and Impact of Corporate Average Fuel Economy (CAFE) Standards. In 2000, he was appointed a fellow of the California Council on Science and Technology and was elected a senior fellow of the U.S. Association for Energy Economics in 1999. He won an Excellence in Teaching Award from the Stanford Society of Black Scientists and Engineers in 1989 and the Federal Energy Administration Distinguished Service Award in 1975. He earned a bachelor's degree in electrical engineering from the Massachusetts Institute of Technology in 1966 and a doctoral degree in engineering-economic systems from Stanford University in 1971.

John B. Taylor
GEORGE P. SHULTZ SENIOR FELLOW IN ECONOMICS
CHAIR, WORKING GROUP ON ECONOMIC POLICY
MEMBER OF THE TASK FORCE ON ENERGY POLICY

John B. Taylor is the George P. Shultz Senior Fellow in Economics at the Hoover Institution and the Mary and Robert Raymond Professor of Economics at Stanford University. He was previously the director of the Stanford Institute for Economic Policy Research and was founding director of Stanford's Introductory Economics Center. He has a long and distinguished record of public service. Among other roles, he served as a member of the President's Council of Economic Advisors from 1989 to 1991 and as undersecretary of the treasury for international affairs from 2001 to 2005. He is currently a member of the California Governor's Council of Economic Advisors.

David G. Victor
MEMBER OF THE TASK FORCE ON ENERGY POLICY

David G. Victor is a professor at the University of California, San Diego, in the School of International Relations and Pacific Studies and director of the Laboratory on International Law and Regulation. Previously, he ran Stanford University's Program on Energy and Sustainable Development and was a professor at Stanford Law School. His current research examines when and how international law works. His books include *Natural Gas and Geopolitics* (Cambridge University Press, 2006) and *The Collapse of the Kyoto Protocol* (Princeton University Press, 2001, 2004). He received his AB from Harvard and his PhD from the Massachusetts Institute of Technology in political science.

R. James Woolsey
MEMBER OF THE TASK FORCE ON ENERGY POLICY

R. James Woolsey was the Annenberg Distinguished Visiting Fellow at the Hoover Institution at Stanford University, 2008–09; currently he is a venture partner at VantagePoint Venture Partners; a senior executive adviser to Booz Allen Hamilton; counsel to the law firm of Goodwin Procter; and chairman of the Strategic Advisory Group of Paladin Capital Group.

Jeremy Carl, Research Manager

Jeremy Carl is a PhD candidate in the Interdisciplinary Program in Environment and Resources and a research Fellow with the Program on Energy and Sustainable Development at Stanford University. Mr. Carl previously worked with The Energy and Resources Institute (TERI) of New Delhi, India, on energy and resource economics and served as a staff member at Environmental Defense. He received his BA with distinction in history from Yale University and an MPA from the John F. Kennedy School of Government, Harvard University.

APPENDIX 3

CONFERENCE AGENDA

January 19–20, 2010
Hoover Institution
Stanford University

Participants

Members of the Shultz-Stephenson Task Force on Energy Policy and distinguished invited experts in energy-related fields

Purpose

To discuss seven critical energy issues that could be favorably influenced by effective public policies at the state, local, and federal level.

Where do these key energy issues stand in light of the past year's executive branch and congressional efforts and international developments? What is going right, what needs correcting, where are the gaps, what must be done to optimize policies?

DAY ONE: NEW APPROACHES TO LEGACY ISSUES

8:30 A.M. **Continental Breakfast**

9:00 A.M. **Welcome**

John Raisian, director and senior fellow, Hoover Institution

9:10 A.M. **Introduction: A Conversation on Major Trends in Energy Developments**

> *George Shultz*, *distinguished fellow and Energy Task Force chair, Hoover Institution; former secretary of state, and* **Burton Richter**, *former director, SLAC National Accelerator Laboratory, and Hoover Institution Energy Task Force member*

10:00 A.M. **Break**

10:15 A.M. **Session I: Distributed Energy**

What policy framework(s) would be necessary to increase the adoption of distributed energy technologies?

> *Moderator:* **James Boyd**, *vice chair, California Energy Commission*
> *Speaker:* **R. James Woolsey**, *former distinguished visiting fellow and Energy Task Force member, Hoover Institution; former director of Central Intelligence*
> *Discussant:* **Dan Reicher**, *director, Climate and Energy Initiatives, Google.org*

12:00 P.M. **Lunch**

1:00 P.M. **Session II: What Can We Do to Boost Energy Efficiency?**

How can we use legislation, regulation, or incentives to promote behavioral change so that energy efficiency no longer underfulfills its potential?

> *Moderator:* **John Weyant**, *professor, Department of Management Science and Engineering, Stanford University*
> *Speaker:* **Jim Sweeney**, *senior fellow and Energy Task Force member, Hoover Institution; director, Precourt Institute for Energy Efficiency, Stanford University*

*Discussant: **Jonathan Koomey**, consulting professor, civil and environmental engineering, Stanford University*

2:30 P.M.   **Break**

2:45 P.M.   **Session III: Addressing the Nuclear Fuel Cycle**

Internationalizing enrichment services and solving the problem of spent fuel storage

*Moderator: **Robert Rosner**, distinguished service professor, Physics and Astronomy & Astrophysics, University of Chicago, visiting professor, Center for International Security and Cooperation, Stanford University and former director, Argonne National Laboratory*
*Speaker: **Ellen Tauscher**, undersecretary of state for arms control and international security, State Department*
*Discussant: **Tom Isaacs**, consulting professor, Center for International Security and Cooperation, Stanford University and director, Planning and Special Studies, Lawrence Livermore National Laboratory*

5:00 P.M.   **Conference Adjourns**

6:30 P.M.   **Reception**

7:00 P.M.   **Evening Discussion and Dinner**

(Open to invited guests)

A Conversation with Governor Arnold Schwarzenegger

DAY TWO: EMERGING ISSUES IN ENERGY POLICY MAKING

8:30 A.M.   **Continental Breakfast**

9:00 A.M.   **Session IV: Synthetic Biology: Prospects and Issues**

Perspectives on the contribution of synthetic biology to energy needs; governance issues

Moderator: **Paul Berg**, *professor emeritus, Stanford University; Hoover Institution Energy Task Force member*
Speaker: **Craig Venter**, *founder, chairman, CEO, co-chief scientific officer, Synthetic Genomics and founder, chairman, president, J. Craig Venter Institute*
Panelists: **Jay Keasling**, *professor, University of California, Berkeley, and* **Drew Endy**, *Ph.D., president, BioBricks Foundation and assistant professor, Stanford University Bioengineering*

10:45 A.M.   **Break**

11:00 A.M.   **Session V: Putting a Price on Carbon**

Should the United States prefer a revenue-neutral carbon tax or cap-and-trade in our future climate policy? Is a gas tax the best way to reduce carbon in our transportation system?

Moderator: **Roger Noll**, *professor emeritus, Department of Economics, Stanford University*
Speaker: **Larry Goulder**, *professor and chairman, Department of Economics, Stanford University; Hoover Institution Energy Task Force member*
Discussant: **Terry M. Dinan**, *senior adviser, Congressional Budget Office*

12:15 P.M.   **Lunch**

1:15 P.M.   **Session VI: A Sustained Research and Development Policy**

Should we fund dedicated national energy labs or research centers? How can we improve the interface between government R&D and private venture capital?

Moderator: **Sidney Drell**, *senior fellow and Energy Task Force member, Hoover Institution; former deputy director of SLAC National Accelerator Laboratory*
Speaker: **Arun Majumdar**, *director, Advanced Research Projects Agency-Energy, Department of Energy*
Discussant: **Mike Goguen**, *Sequoia Capital*

2:45 P.M. **Break**

3:00 P.M. **Session VII: Emerging International Energy Relationships and What We Can Do to Make Them Better**

How can the Copenhagen process be managed successfully from the perspective of U.S. economic, security, and environmental interests? Should we be stressing positive and specific goals for step-by-step progress? How can U.S.-China and U.S.-India energy relations be put on a more productive trajectory?

Panel discussion with: **David Victor**, *professor, University of California, San Diego, and Hoover Institution Energy Task Force member (moderator),* **Charles Ebinger**, *director, Energy Security Initiative, Brookings Institution, and* **Michael Wara**, *assistant professor, Stanford Law School*

4:30 P.M. **Conference Summary and Suggested Follow-Up**

What have we learned from our conversations over the past two days? How can this task force help address some of the major policy gaps in U.S. energy policy?

George Shultz and Burton Richter

5:00 P.M. **Conference End**

CONFERENCE PARTICIPANTS

January 19–20, 2010
Hoover Institution
Stanford University

MODERATORS (in order of appearance):

James D. Boyd was appointed to a second five-year term on the California Energy Commission on February 2, 2007, and has served as the vice chair since June 2006. Boyd presides over the Energy Commission's Transportation and Fuels Committee. He oversees the implementation of Assembly Bill 118, which established an Alternative and Renewable Fuel and Vehicle Technology Program at the Energy Commission. Boyd has been involved in Zero Emission Vehicle strategies for more than twenty years. He spent fifteen years as the chief executive officer of the California Air Resources Board (CARB), during which time CARB established new pollution control programs for motor vehicles. Commissioner Boyd chairs the Bioenergy Interagency Working Group that developed and implements Governor Schwarzenegger's Bioenergy Action Plan. He currently leads the commission's efforts to develop the State Alternative Fuels Plan requested by the California governor and legislature. He is the Energy Commission's representative on the Steering Team of the California Fuel Cell Partnership and has served on the governor's Hydrogen Highway Network Implementation Advisory Panel. He presently serves on the governor's Climate Action Team. A California native, Commissioner Boyd received his Bachelor of Science degree in Business Administration from the University of California, Berkeley.

John P. Weyant is professor of Management Science and Engineering, director of the Energy Modeling Forum (EMF), and deputy director of the Precourt Institute for Energy Efficiency at Stanford University. He is also a senior fellow of the Freeman Spogli Institute for International Studies and the Woods Institute for the Environment at Stanford. Professor Weyant earned a BS/MS in Aeronautical Engineering and Astronautics and MS degrees in Engineering Management and in Operations Research and Statistics, all from Rensselaer Polytechnic Institute, and a PhD in Management Science with minors in Economics, Operations Research, and Organization Theory from University of California at Berkeley. He was a National Science Foundation postdoctoral fellow at Harvard's Kennedy School of Government. Weyant has been a convening lead author for the Intergovernmental Panel on Climate Change (IPCC) for chapters on integrated assessment, greenhouse gas mitigation, integrated climate impacts, and sustainable development, and most recently served as a review editor for the climate change mitigation working group of the IPCC's fourth assessment report. Weyant was honored in 2007 as a major contributor to the Nobel Peace Prize awarded to the IPCC and in 2008 by Chairman Mary Nichols for contributions to the California Air Resources Board's Economic and Technology Advancement Advisory Committee on Assembly Bill 32.

Robert Rosner is a visiting professor at Stanford's Center for Security and International Cooperation for 2009–2010. He is the William E. Wrather Distinguished Service Professor in the departments of Astronomy and Astrophysics and Physics at the University of Chicago. Dr. Rosner recently stepped down as director of Argonne National Laboratory, where he had also served as chief scientist. He led the DOE Accelerated Strategic Computing Initiative Flash Center at Chicago for its first five years. This center has been a pioneer in the development of computational astrophysics codes with broad applicability to other disciplines. He is also involved with a University of Wisconsin/Chicago/Princeton University NSF-supported

Physics Frontier Center, which focuses on problems lying at the boundary of astrophysics and laboratory plasma physics, mostly in areas related to magnetohydrodynamic instabilities in low Prandtl number fluids (such as liquid metals or stellar interiors). For the past seven years, he has become heavily involved in issues related to science and technology policy and management, especially in areas related to energy, climate, and modeling and simulations, national security, as well as with national policy issues related to STEM (science, technology, engineering, and math) workforce development, nuclear and renewable energy technology development, and the role of national laboratories in scientific, technological, and industrial competitiveness, including the relationship between national laboratories, academia, and industry.

Paul Berg is widely regarded as one of the principal pioneers in gene splicing. He received his BS from Pennsylvania State University and his PhD in biochemistry from Case Western Reserve University. After serving on the faculty of Washington University in St. Louis, he came to Stanford in 1959, where he chaired the Department of Biochemistry from 1969 to 1974 and served as director of the Beckman Center for Molecular and Genetic Medicine from 1985 to 2000. He served as a director of the foundation for the NIH from 1993 to 2004. Dr. Berg developed the recombinant DNA technology and methods to map the structure and function of DNA. For these achievements, he was awarded the Lasker Basic Science Award, the Annual Award of the Gairdner Foundation, and the Nobel Prize in Chemistry in 1980. In addition, Berg is an elected member of the U.S. National Academy of Sciences, the American Philosophical Society, French Academy of Science, the Royal Society (London) and received the National Medal of Science. Dr. Berg's activities in social and political issues related to genetics research have been nearly as influential as his research itself. The "Berg Letter," calling for a brief cessation in recombinant DNA experimentation, led to the renowned Asilomar Conference in

1975. Dr. Berg continues to shape the public debate on stem cell research, biotechnology, and human cloning. Dr. Berg currently serves on the Hoover Institution's Shultz-Stephenson Task Force on Energy Policy.

Roger G. Noll is professor of economics emeritus at Stanford University and a senior fellow at the Stanford Institute for Economic Policy Research. Before coming to Stanford, Noll was a senior economist at the President's Council of Economic Advisers, a senior fellow at the Brookings Institution, and Institute Professor of Social Science at the California Institute of Technology. Noll is the author of over three hundred publications. Noll's research interests include technology policy; antitrust, regulation and privatization; the economic approach to administrative law; and the economics of sports. Noll has been a member of the advisory boards of the U.S. Department of Energy, Jet Propulsion Laboratory, National Aeronautics and Space Administration, National Renewable Energy Laboratory, and National Science Foundation.

Sidney D. Drell is a Senior Fellow at the Hoover Institution and professor of theoretical physics (emeritus) at the SLAC National Accelerator Laboratory, Stanford University. He is a member of JASON, a group of academic scientists who consult for the government on issues of national importance, a member of the governing boards of LANS and LLNS, the LLCs that currently manage the Los Alamos and Livermore National Laboratories. He has served as a member of the President's Foreign Intelligence Advisory Board and on a number of advisory bodies to the Congress and Intelligence Community. Dr. Drell currently serves on the Hoover Institution's Shultz-Stephenson Task Force on Energy Policy.

David Victor is a professor at the School of International Relations and Pacific Studies and director of the school's new Laboratory on International Law and Regulation. Looking across a wide array of issues from environment and energy to human rights, trade, and security, the laboratory explores when (and why) international laws actually work. Most recently, Victor served as director of the Program on Energy and Sustainable Development at the Freeman Spogli Institute for International Studies at Stanford University, where he was also a professor at Stanford Law School. Previously, he directed the science and technology program at the Council on Foreign Relations (CFR) in New York, where he directed the council's task force on energy, co-chaired by Jim Schlesinger and John Deutch and was senior adviser to the task force on climate change, chaired by governors George Pataki and Tom Vilsack. Victor's research at Stanford and CFR examined ways to improve management of the nation's $50 billion strategic oil reserve, strategies for managing investment in "geoengineering," and a wide array of other topics related to technological innovation and the impact of innovation on economic growth. His research also examined global forest policy, global warming, and genetic engineering of food crops. He currently serves on the Hoover Institution's Shultz-Stephenson Task Force on Energy Policy.

SPEAKERS (in order of appearance):

George P. Shultz, the Thomas W. and Susan B. Ford Distinguished Fellow at the Hoover Institution, has had a distinguished career in government, in academia, and in business. He is a professor (emeritus) in Stanford University's Graduate School of Business and has held four different cabinet posts, most notably as secretary of state (1982–1989). He also served as secretary of labor and the treasury, was director of the Office of Management and Budget, and was president and director of the Bechtel Group, Inc. He currently chairs the Hoover Institution's Shultz-Stephenson Task Force on Energy Policy.

Burton Richter is a Nobel Prize winner (Physics, 1976). He is Paul Pigott Professor in the Physical Sciences emeritus, Stanford University; former director, SLAC National Accelerator Center; member, National Academy of Sciences; fellow, American Academy of Arts and Sciences, American Philosophical Society, and American Association for the Advancement of Science; former president, American Physical Society and the International Union of Pure and Applied Physics. For the last ten years he has spent most of his time on energy issues and is currently a member of the DOE's Nuclear Energy Advisory Committee, chairing its subcommittee on Advanced Fuel Cycles. He chaired the influential 2008 American Physical Society's Energy Efficiency study; is on the Advisory Council of the Precourt Energy Efficiency Center, Stanford University; and is a member of the JASON Group, and the French Atomic Energy Commission (CEA) external science and technology Visiting Group. Dr. Richter currently serves on the Hoover Institution's Shultz-Stephenson Task Force on Energy Policy.

R. James Woolsey is the former Annenberg Distinguished Visiting Fellow at the Hoover Institution at Stanford University; a venture partner at VantagePoint Venture Partners; counsel to the law firm of Goodwin Procter; and chairman of the Strategic Advisory Group of Paladin Capital Group. Prior to VantagePoint, Woolsey was a partner with Booz Allen Hamilton, specializing in energy and security issues and a partner with Shea & Gardner, specializing in commercial litigation and alternative dispute resolution. He practiced at the firm on four different occasions for a total of twenty-two years. Woolsey served five times in the federal government for a total of twelve years, holding presidential appointments in two Democratic and two Republican administrations. He served as director of Central Intelligence (1993–95), ambassador and chief negotiator for the Conventional Armed Forces in Europe Treaty in Vienna (1989–91), delegate at large (part-time) to the Strategic Arms Reduction Talks and the Defense and Space Talks in Geneva (1983–86), undersecretary of the navy (1977–79), and general counsel to the U.S. Senate Committee on Armed Services (1970–73). Woolsey received his BA degree from Stanford University (1963, with great distinction, Phi Beta Kappa), an MA from Oxford University (Rhodes Scholar, 1963–65), and an LLB from Yale Law School (1968, managing editor of the *Yale Law Journal*). He currently serves on the Hoover Institution's Shultz-Stephenson Task Force on Energy Policy.

James L. Sweeney is a professor of management science and engineering at Stanford University, where he was appointed to the faculty in 1971. He also is a senior fellow at the Stanford Institute for Economic Policy Research and at the Hoover Institution. At Stanford, Sweeney was chairman, Department of Engineering-Economic Systems & Operations Research, 1996–98; chairman, Department of Engineering-Economic Systems, 1991–96; director, Center for Economic Policy Research, 1984–86; chairman, Institute for Energy Studies, 1981–85; and director, Energy Modeling Forum, 1978–84. He recently served on the review panel for the State of California Public Interest Energy Research Program, on the National Research Council's Committee on Benefits of DOE R&D in Energy Efficiency and Fossil Energy, and on the National Research Council's Committee on Effectiveness and Impact of Corporate Average Fuel Economy (CAFE) Standards. In 2000, Sweeney was appointed a fellow of the California Council on Science and Technology. He was elected a senior fellow of the U.S. Association for Energy Economics in 1999. He won an Excellence in Teaching Award from the Stanford Society of Black Scientists and Engineers in 1989 and the Federal Energy Administration Distinguished Service Award in 1975. Sweeney earned a bachelor's degree in electrical engineering from the Massachusetts Institute of Technology in 1966 and a doctoral degree in engineering-economic systems from Stanford University in 1971. He currently serves on the Hoover Institution's Shultz-Stephenson Task Force on Energy Policy.

Ellen O. Tauscher was sworn in as undersecretary of state for arms control and international security on June 27, 2009. Undersecretary Tauscher previously had represented California's 10th Congressional District for 13 years in the U.S. House of Representatives. The district includes San Francisco's suburbs in Contra Costa, Alameda, Solano, and Sacramento counties. She was the only member of Congress to have two national defense laboratories, Lawrence Livermore and Sandia California, in her district. The district also includes Camp Parks Army Reserve facility and Travis Air Force Base, home of the 60th Air Mobility Wing. She chaired the House Armed Services Subcommittee on Strategic Forces from 2007 to 2009, and she was a senior member of the House Committee on Transportation and Infrastructure. She also chaired the New Democrat Coalition, a group of more than sixty centrist House Democrats. Before winning a seat in Congress, Undersecretary Tauscher spent fourteen years working on Wall Street. She was one of the first women to hold a seat on the New York Stock Exchange and later served as an officer of the American Stock Exchange.

J. Craig Venter, PhD, is founder, chairman, and president of the J. Craig Venter Institute (JCVI), a not-for-profit research organization with approximately 400 scientists and staff dedicated to human, microbial, plant, and environmental genomic research, the exploration of social and ethical issues in genomics, and seeking alternative energy solutions through genomics. Dr. Venter is also founder and CEO of Synthetic Genomics Inc., a privately held company dedicated to commercializing genomic-driven solutions to address global energy and environmental challenges. Dr. Venter has been a driving force in genomics for several decades. The many discoveries and breakthroughs by him and his teams include Expressed Sequence Tags (ESTs), used to rapidly discover new genes, the first draft of the human genome in 2001, the first complete diploid human genome in 2007, more than 20 million new genes from his

Sorcerer II Global Expedition, and groundbreaking advances in creating the first synthetic genome. Dr. Venter is a member of the National Academy of Sciences and was awarded the 2008 National Medal of Science by President Obama.

Lawrence H. Goulder is Shuzo Nishihara Professor in Environmental and Resource Economics, chair of the Economics Department at Stanford University, Kennedy-Grossman Fellow in Human Biology at Stanford, a senior fellow at Stanford's Institute for Economic Policy Research, a research associate at the National Bureau of Economic Research, and University Fellow of Resources for the Future, a nonprofit environmental and natural resource research firm located in Washington, DC. Goulder graduated from Harvard College with an AB in philosophy in 1973. He obtained a master's degree in musical composition from the Ecole Normale de Musique de Paris in 1975 and earned a PhD in economics from Stanford in 1982. He was a faculty member in the Department of Economics at Harvard before returning to Stanford's economics department in 1989. Goulder has conducted analyses for several government agencies, environmental organizations, and industry groups. At Stanford Goulder teaches undergraduate and graduate courses in environmental economics and policy and co-organizes a weekly seminar in applied microeconomics. He currently serves on the Hoover Institution's Shultz-Stephenson Task Force on Energy Policy.

Arun Majumdar became the first director of the Advanced Research Projects Agency-Energy (ARPA-E), the country's only agency devoted to transformational energy research and development, in October 2009. Prior to joining ARPA-E, Majumdar was the Associate Laboratory Director for Energy and Environment at Lawrence Berkeley National Laboratory and a professor of Mechanical Engineering and Materials Science and Engineering at the University of California, Berkeley. His highly distinguished research career includes the science and engineering of energy conversion, transport, and storage, ranging from the molecular and nanoscale levels to large energy systems. In 2005, Majumdar was elected a member of the National Academy of Engineering for this pioneering work. At Berkeley Labs and UC Berkeley, Majumdar helped shape several strategic initiatives in the areas of energy efficiency, renewable energy, and energy storage. He also testified before Congress on how to reduce energy consumption in buildings. Majumdar has also served on the advisory committee of the National Science Foundation's engineering directorate, was a member of the advisory council to the materials sciences and engineering division of the Department of Energy's Basic Energy Sciences, and was an advisor on nanotechnology to the President's Council of Advisors on Science and Technology. Additionally, Majumdar—also an entrepreneur—has served as an advisor to start-up companies and venture capital firms in the Silicon Valley. He received his bachelor's degree in Mechanical Engineering at the Indian Institute of Technology, Bombay, in 1985 and his PhD from the University of California, Berkeley in 1989.

Charles Ebinger is the director of the Energy Security Initiative at the Brookings Institution. Prior to joining Brookings, he was a Senior Energy Advisor at the International Resources Group. Ebinger was an adjunct professor at Georgetown University's School of Foreign Service from 1979 to 2003 and again from 2007 to 2008 and is currently an adjunct professor at Johns Hopkins University's Nitze School of Advanced International Studies. He serves as vice president on the board of directors of the Washington chapter of the International Association of Energy Economists. Dr. Ebinger has thirty years of experience addressing the security, political, economic, environmental, and foreign policy interrelationships surrounding domestic and international energy issues. During his career Dr. Ebinger has advised over sixty governments on restructuring their state-owned energy companies and establishing regulatory regimes. In 1975, he helped to establish the International Energy Agency and its oil-sharing mechanism. From 1976 to 1979,

Dr. Ebinger served as vice president of Conant and Associates, an international oil, gas, and electricity political-risk consulting company. In 1979, he became the founding director of the Center for Strategic and International Studies' Energy and Strategic Resources Program and served as director until 1987. From 1987 to 1988, he was a senior consultant at Putnam Hayes & Bartlett. From 1988 to 1999, he served as executive vice president at the International Resources Group. In 1999, he joined Stone & Webster Management Consultants as the director of its International Energy Practice. From 2000 to 2004, he held several positions at Bechtel Consulting, including Vice President and Director of International Utility Services; Senior Vice President for Middle East, Central Asia, and Africa; and Senior Vice President for Global Privatization/ Restructuring/Regulation. In 2004, he returned to the International Resources Group as a senior advisor, where he worked on restructuring the energy sectors of Nepal, Afghanistan, and Liberia. He received his BA from Williams College, Phi Beta Kappa, and his PhD from the Fletcher School of International Law and Diplomacy at Tufts University, where he graduated first in his class.

Michael Wara is an expert on environmental law and policy. Professor Wara's research focuses on climate policy and regulation, both domestic and international. Wara's current scholarship addresses the performance of the emerging global market for greenhouse gases and mechanisms for reducing emissions, especially in developing countries after the Kyoto Protocol expires in 2012. Professor Wara joined Stanford Law School in 2007 as a research fellow in environmental law and as a lecturer in law. Previously, he was an associate in a large national law firm, where his practice focused on climate change, land use, and environmental law. Professor Wara received his JD from Stanford Law School, his PhD in ocean sciences from the University of California at Santa Cruz, and his BA from Columbia University.

DISCUSSANTS (in order of appearance):

Dan Reicher is the director of Climate Change and Energy Initiatives at Google. Prior to Google Mr. Reicher worked for and had been involved with the Obama Transition Team, New Energy Capital, Northern Power, World Resources Institute, U.S. Department of Energy, Natural Resources Defense Council, U.S. Department of Justice, and President's Commission on the Accident at Three Mile Island. He holds a BA in Biology from Dartmouth College and a JD from Stanford Law School. Additionally, he has studied at Harvard and the Massachusetts Institute of Technology.

Jonathan Koomey is a project scientist at Lawrence Berkeley National Laboratory, a consulting professor at Stanford University, and was (for the Autumn semester of 2009) a visiting professor at Yale University's School of Forestry and Environmental Studies. Dr. Koomey holds MS and PhD degrees from the Energy and Resources Group at UC Berkeley and an AB in history of science from Harvard University. He is the author or coauthor of eight books and more than 150 articles and reports on energy efficiency and power technologies, energy economics, energy policy, environmental externalities, global climate change, and critical thinking skills, and is one of the leading international experts on the economics of reducing greenhouse gas emissions and the effects of information technology on resource use.

Tom Isaacs is a consulting professor at Stanford University's Center for Security and International Cooperation. He is also the director of Planning and Special Studies at Lawrence Livermore National Laboratory. He is a member of the National Academy of Sciences Nuclear and Radiation Studies Board. Mr. Isaacs focuses on issues at the intersection of nuclear power, nonproliferation, and waste management and on issues of earning public trust and confidence.

He has had extensive experience in the federal government. He was director of the Office of Geologic Repositories in DOE, deputy director of the DOE Office of Safeguards and Security, and director of the Instability and Insurgency Center in the Central Intelligence Agency.

Jay Keasling received his BS in chemistry and biology from the University of Nebraska in 1986, his PhD in chemical engineering from the University of Michigan in 1991, and did postdoctoral work in biochemistry at Stanford University from 1991 to 1992. Keasling joined the Department of Chemical Engineering at the University of California, Berkeley as an assistant professor in 1992, where he is currently the Hubbard Howe Distinguished Professor of Biochemical Engineering. Keasling is also a professor in the Department of Bioengineering at Berkeley, a senior faculty scientist and acting deputy director of the Lawrence Berkeley National Laboratory, and chief executive officer of the Joint Bioenergy Institute. Dr. Keasling's research focuses on engineering microorganisms for environmentally friendly synthesis of small molecules or degradation of environmental contaminants. Keasling's laboratory has engineered bacteria and yeast to produce polymers, a precursor to the antimalarial drug artemisinin, and advanced biofuels and soil microorganisms to accumulate uranium and to degrade nerve agents.

Drew Endy, PhD, recently joined the faculty of bioengineering at Stanford University, having previously helped to build the Department of Biological Engineering at MIT. He serves as president of the nonprofit BioBricks Foundation and has cofounded three companies, two of which have not yet failed. He helped start the Registry of Standard Biological Parts, iGEM—a worldwide genetic engineering "Olympics" for undergraduates—and the BIOFAB—a public-benefit production facility producing free-to-use standard biological parts.

Terry Dinan is Senior Advisor for Climate Issues at the Congressional Budget Office. Before joining CBO, she was an economist at the Environmental Protection Agency and at Oak Ridge National Laboratory. She has published in a variety of professional journals, including the National Tax Journal, the Journal of Environmental Economics and Management, and the Journal of Urban Economics. She served as an associate editor for the Journal of Environmental Economics and Management, was on the board of directors for the Association of Environmental and Resource Economists, and has testified before Congress on issues associated with the design of climate change policy. She has a PhD in economics from Iowa State University.

Michael Goguen is a venture capitalist at Sequoia Capital focusing on cleantech, semiconductor, and systems investments. Prior to joining Sequoia Capital in 1996, Mr. Goguen spent ten years in various engineering, research, and product management roles at DEC, SynOptics, and Centillion, and was a director of engineering at Bay Networks (NT). He was also a technical chairman of the Asynchronous Transfer Mode Forum. He has a BS in electrical engineering from Cornell University and an MS in electrical engineering from Stanford University.

PARTICIPANTS:

Steve Bechtel is chairman retired and director of Bechtel Group, Inc. He is also chairman emeritus and director of Fremont Group, LLC. In addition, Mr. Bechtel is chairman of the S.D. Bechtel, Jr., Foundation and the Stephen Bechtel Fund. Mr. Bechtel's business headquarters are in San Francisco. He served several industry and community organizations as chairman, including the Business Council, the Conference Board, Inc., and the National Academy of Engineering. He served as vice chairman on the California Council for Science and Technology Task Force to advise Governor

Schwarzenegger on improving K-12 science and mathematics education. Mr. Bechtel currently serves on the Shultz-Stephenson Task Force on Energy Policy and the MIT Energy Initiative External Advisory Board.

Sally M. Benson is director of the Global Climate and Energy Project and a professor (research) in the Department of Energy Resources Engineering at Stanford University. She received her BA from Barnard College in geology and her MS and PhD from the University of California. Prior to joining Stanford, Benson worked at Lawrence Berkeley National Laboratory as Division Director for Earth Sciences, Associate Laboratory Director for Energy Sciences, and Deputy Director for Operations. Benson works on carbon dioxide capture and sequestration in deep underground geological formations. Benson was a coordinating lead author on the 2005 Intergovernmental Panel on Climate Change Special Report on Carbon Dioxide Capture and Storage. She also serves on the boards of directors of the National Renewable Energy Laboratory and Climate Central.

Warren Belmar, managing director of Capitol Counsel Group, LLC, is a retired partner with the law firm of Fulbright & Jaworski, LLP, who served from June 2006 through January 2009 as the Deputy General Counsel for Energy Policy of the U.S. Department of Energy (DOE). In that role, he acted as principal legal advisor, on behalf of the general counsel, to the secretary and senior DOE officials within assigned functional areas, including the development and regulatory implementation of the department's Loan Guarantee Program for Innovative Technologies and its Advanced Technology Vehicle Loan Program, resolving issues arising in the operation of the department's energy efficiency, alternative fuels, and renewable energy programs and in the department's efforts to address electric transmission congestion matters and to facilitate the construction of wind, solar, hydro, geothermal and other renewable energy sources for electric power generation. Mr. Belmar currently serves as chair of the Federal Clean Energy Finance Committee of the American

Bar Association's Section of Administrative Law and Regulatory Practice and as a member of the board of the Clean Economy Network Foundation.

Tara Billingsley is the staff economist for the Senate Committee on Energy and Natural Resources (majority staff). She covers economic and energy security issues for the committee, from upstream international geopolitical issues to downstream price and supply issues. She worked on several key portions of the Energy Independence and Security Act of 2007 and the Energy Policy Act of 2005. Prior to joining the committee, Ms. Billingsley worked at the Department of Energy in a variety of roles, including briefing the secretary of energy on energy security issues. Ms. Billingsley has also worked for the Royal Institute of International Affairs' Energy and Environmental Program in London. She holds undergraduate and graduate degrees in international affairs and energy economics from the American University School of International Service and the Johns Hopkins School of Advanced International Studies.

Chaim Braun is a consulting professor at the Center for International Security and Cooperation in Stanford University, where he conducts studies related to nuclear energy growth and related possible proliferation spread in the Middle East, Central Asia, South Asia, and South America. Chaim Braun has thirty-five years of management and consulting experience in the electric and nuclear power industry, emphasizing domestic and international power plant economics and international nuclear power nonproliferation issues, particularly related to the United States, East Asia, and Eastern Europe. Chaim coined the term "proliferation rings" and developed a concept for providing incentives to reduce the demand for weapons of mass desctruction, including the concepts of assured nuclear fuel supplies and nuclear fuel banks. Mr. Braun has worked on reviewing the implementation plans for UNSC Resolution 1540 and the support roles of regional organizations and industrial corporations.

John Burges is managing director and head of energy at Knight Capital Markets, the largest securities trading institution in North America. He previously worked at Deutsche Bank and Merrill Lynch as a director in their energy investment banking practice. He was chairman of Newmarket Power, LLC, a private equity-backed independent power company with 450 megawatts of gas-fired power generation. He was co-head of a private equity investment company based in the Middle East that invested across the energy spectrum including in the solar sector. He has founded various renewable energy advocacy groups, including the Alliance for Renewable Energy and its Florida chapter FARE. John has an MBA from Columbia Business School and a BA (Hons) from Bristol University, England.

Persis S. Drell is professor and director at SLAC National Accelerator Laboratory, Stanford University. She joined the faculty of the Physics Department at Cornell University in 1988. In 2002, Dr. Drell accepted a position as professor and director of research at SLAC. In 2005, Dr. Drell was named deputy director of SLAC and director of Particle and Particle Astrophysics. She was appointed director in December 2007. Dr. Drell has been the recipient of a Guggenheim Fellowship and a National Science Foundation Presidential Young Investigator Award and is a fellow of the American Physical Society. She chaired the High Energy Physics Advisory Panel subcommittee that produced the "Quantum Universe" report, and in spring of 2006 she was the Morris Loeb Lecturer in Physics at Harvard University.

Putnam M. Ebinger received her BA degree in history from Sweet Briar College and her MA, MALD, and PhD in International Affairs from the Fletcher School of Law and Diplomacy at Tufts University. Over a twenty-year career at the School of Foreign Service at Georgetown University, she served as director of the Bachelor of

Science in Foreign Service Program, senior academic dean, and finally vice dean. In these capacities, she worked across departments and degree programs to establish a wide range of regional, multidisciplinary, and joint degree programs, including the German and European Studies Program and the major in Science, Technology, and International Affairs.

Robert H. Edwards, Jr., is the Deputy General Counsel for Energy Policy of the Department of Energy. In this capacity he provides legal and policy advice to the Office of Energy Efficiency and Renewable Energy; Office of Electricity Delivery and Energy Reliability; and the Office of Fossil Energy. He also works closely with the Recovery Act Team. Mr. Edwards has practiced law in Washington, DC, for twenty years. He has extensive experience advising equity investors, sponsors, lenders, governments, and other projects participants in the development and financing of energy, infrastructure, and renewable energy projects in the United States and around the globe. He has represented clients in Asia, Africa, Eastern Europe, and Latin America in energy and infrastructure public-private partnerships, energy sector restructuring, and privatization. Mr. Edwards graduated magna cum laude with an AB in economics from Harvard University. He earned a Master of Business Administration degree from the Stanford Graduate School of Business and a Juris Doctor degree from Stanford Law School, where he served as an associate managing editor of the *Stanford Journal of International Law.*

Ed Frank is a vice president at Apple Corporation, where he is responsible for Macintosh computer hardware engineering. Prior to joining Apple, he spent ten years at Broadcom Corporation, most recently as Corporate Vice President of Research and Development, following the acquisition of Epigram, a company he cofounded in 1996. Earlier in his career he was a Distinguished Engineer at Sun Microsystems, where he was a principal of the Green Project, which created what ultimately became the Java programming language. Dr. Frank is a Life Trustee of Carnegie Mellon University and serves as the chairman of its capital campaign. He also serves on the board of directors of several early-stage start-ups and is a Technology Partner with Advanced Technology Ventures, a Palo Alto based venture capital firm. Dr. Frank holds BSEE and MSEE degrees from Stanford University and a PhD in Computer Science from Carnegie Mellon University. He is a named inventor on more than forty patents.

Paul Gipe has written extensively about renewable energy for both the popular and trade press. His most recent book, *Wind Energy Basics: A Guide to Home- and Community-scale Wind Energy Systems*, is available from Chelsea Green Publishing. In 2004, Gipe launched a campaign to bring electricity-feed laws back to North America. The campaign has grown into a continent-wide grassroots movement that has put renewable energy feed-in tariffs on the political agenda in Canada and the United States.

James E. Goodby is an author and former U.S. diplomat. He graduated from Harvard in 1951 and served as a second lieutenant in the U.S. Air Force during the Korean War. He later served as a U.S. Foreign Service officer, a position he filled in various roles until his retirement in 1989. Some highlights during this period include negotiations with NATO alliance partners as part of the Conference on Security and Cooperation in Europe to create the Helsinki Accords. Mr. Goodby also served as the U.S. ambassador to Finland in 1980 and 1981 and also as vice chairman of the U.S. delegation to the Strategic Arms Reduction Talks (START). In 1993 he returned from retirement to become the chief U.S. negotiator for the Safe and Secure Dismantlement of Nuclear Weapons. During this time he negotiated agreements with several former Soviet republics to dismantle former Soviet nuclear weapons and to prevent nuclear weapons proliferation. He later won the first annual Heinz Award for this work. He currently is a nonresident senior fellow of the

Center for Northeast Asian Policy Studies at the Brookings Institute, a member of the Bipartisan Security Group and a research fellow at the Hoover Institution, Stanford University. He currently serves on the Hoover Institution's Shultz-Stephenson Task Force on Energy Policy.

Brian C. Griffin has held numerous senior-level positions in both the public and private sectors. His distinguished public service career includes serving as a senior government official under three presidents and as both an energy and environmental cabinet secretary under two governors. In the private sector, he has served as both the executive vice president and general counsel of a New York Stock Exchange–listed oil and gas exploration company and previously served as the president of Clean Energy Systems, Inc. Dr. Griffin received his undergraduate degree from Harvard University in 1974 and was selected as a Rhodes Scholar. As a Rhodes Scholar, he attended Oxford University, where he received his British law degree. He also holds an American Juris Doctor degree. As a well-known energy and environmental expert, Dr. Griffin has lectured around the world on topics including conventional and alternative energy technologies, energy utilization and its environmental impacts, as well as national energy security.

Steven F. Hayward is the F.K. Weyerhaeuser Fellow at the American Enterprise Institute (AEI) in Washington, DC, where he writes AEI's regular newsletter *Environmental Policy Outlook*, and is also senior fellow at the Pacific Research Institute for Public Policy in San Francisco. He holds a PhD in American Studies and an MA in government from Claremont Graduate University in California. He is the author of five books on American politics and policy and writes frequently on a wide range of current topics, including environmentalism, law, economics, and public policy for publications including *National Review*, *Weekly Standard*, *Public Interest*, the *Claremont Review of Books*, and *Policy Review*.

Siegfried Hecker is a professor (research) in the Department of Management Science and Engineering at Stanford University, a senior fellow at Freeman Spogli Institute, and codirector of the Center for Security and International Cooperation. He is also an emeritus director of Los Alamos National Laboratory. Hecker's research interests include plutonium science, nuclear weapon policy and international security, nuclear security (including nonproliferation and counterterrorism), and cooperative nuclear threat reduction. Over the past fifteen years, he has fostered cooperation with the Russian nuclear laboratories to secure and safeguard the vast stockpile of ex-Soviet fissile materials. His current interests include the challenges of nuclear India, Pakistan, North Korea, and the nuclear aspirations of Iran. Hecker works closely with the Russian Academy of Sciences and is actively involved with the U.S. National Academies, serving as a member of the National Academies Committee on International Security and Arms Control Nonproliferation Panel.

Hillard Huntington is executive director of Stanford University's Energy Modeling Forum, which received the prestigious Adelman-Frankel Award in 2005. His interests include modeling energy markets and policy decisions. He is a senior fellow and a past president of the United States Association for Energy Economics and a member of the National Petroleum Council. He has served as vice president for publications for the International Association for Energy Economics, as a member of the American Statistical Association's Committee on Energy Data, and on a joint USA-Russia National Academy of Sciences panel on energy conservation research and development. Huntington has testified before the U.S. Senate Committee on Foreign Relations on energy security issues. Prior to coming to Stanford in 1980, he held positions in the corporate and government sectors.

Kenneth Judd is the Paul H. Bauer Senior Fellow at the Hoover Institution. He is an expert in the economies of taxation, imperfect competition, and mathematical economies. His current research focuses on tax policy and antitrust issues, as well as on developing computational methods for economic modeling. A fellow of the Econometric Society, he is coeditor of the *Journal of Economic Dynamics and Control*, associate editor of the *Economics Bulletin*, and associate editor of *Computational Economics*. He currently serves on the Hoover Institution's Shultz-Stephenson Task Force on Energy Policy.

Alexander A. Karsner served as America's ninth assistant secretary for Energy Efficiency and Renewable Energy (EERE), from 2005 to 2008, a period of unprecedented growth in clean energy technologies, investments, and policy formulations. He distinguished himself as a principal architect of and contributor to international climate change deliberations toward achieving a post-2012 global energy framework and as America's top regulator for energy efficiency. Mr. Karsner brings twenty years of experience in global energy development and project financing across a wide array of conventional and renewable sources. Previously, he served as CEO of the power development and consulting firm Enercorp and both director and senior development manager for Wartsila Diesel. Mr. Karsner is currently on the board of directors of Argonne National Laboratory, Conservation International, and Applied Materials, the world's leading nanomanufacturer. He is a Distinguished Fellow at the Council on Competitiveness and a leader of the Energy Future Coalition. He currently serves on the Hoover Institution's Shultz-Stephenson Task Force on Energy Policy.

Ron Kent is the Strategic Technologies RD&D manager for the Sempra Energy Utilities—Southern California Gas Company and San Diego Gas & Electric. In this capacity, Mr. Kent helps to develop and commercialize new energy technologies that minimize energy consumption, emissions, climate impacts, and water consumption. His current projects include the development of a wide variety of innovative new technologies, including oxy-fuel power plants for carbon capture and sequestration, digester gas clean-up, petcoke and biomass gasification, algae energy cycles, microbial generators, advanced microwave devices, chiller and flue gas energy and water conservation, and smart systems for building fault detection, diagnostics and optimization.

Suzi Kerr is a visiting professor in the Economics Department at Stanford University and a senior research associate in Stanford's Program in Energy and Sustainable Development. She is also a senior fellow at Motu Economic and Public Policy Research in New Zealand. Kerr graduated from Harvard University in 1995 with a PhD in Economics and was an assistant professor at the University of Maryland–College Park. From 1999 to 2009 Kerr cofounded and was director of Motu. She has been a visiting scholar at Resources for the Future (USA) and in the Joint Center for the Science and Policy of Global Change at MIT. Her research work focuses on emissions trading for land-use related emissions in both the tropics and New Zealand and nutrient trading to manage water quality. Kerr is involved at a high level in climate policy in New Zealand.

Rachel Kleinfeld is the cofounder and CEO of the Truman National Security Project, an organization dedicated to building the next generation of progressive leaders in national security. Rachel's work focuses on issues at the interstices of national security, human security, and development. Previously, as a senior consultant at Booz Allen Hamilton, Rachel worked on energy security, terrorism, homeland security, and trade and security issues. As a consultant at the Center for Strategic and International Studies, she has written with the Honorable Richard Danzig on citizen preparedness for bioterrorism. Ms. Kleinfeld has consulted for the World Bank and multiple government agencies and private organizations on building the rule of law in weak states. She has worked in human rights and economic development in India, Israel, and Eastern Europe, and has served as an elections monitor in Pakistan and Bangladesh. Ms. Kleinfeld's commentary has been published in multiple books, magazines, and newspapers; she has also served as a regular blogger for *National Journal*'s security experts blog and the *New York Times* during the 2008 campaign. A Rhodes Scholar and Truman Scholar, Rachel received her BA from Yale University and her MPhil and DPhil in International Relations from St. Antony's College, Oxford.

Lee Lane is a resident fellow at the American Enterprise Institute (AEI) and codirector of AEI's Geoengineering Project. Lane recently coauthored "An Analysis of Climate Engineering as a Response to Climate Change," published by the Copenhagen Consensus Center, and "Institutions for Developing New Climate Solutions," to be published by the World Federation of Scientists. He is also the author of *Strategic Options for Bush Administration Climate Policy* (AEI Press, November 2006). Lane has been a consultant to the U.S. departments of Energy, Transportation, and State, as well as to NASA and Japan's Ministry of Economy, Trade, and Industry. He is a consultant with Charles River Associates. Before joining AEI, Lane served for seven years as the executive director of the Climate Policy Center in Washington, DC.

Howard Leach is a business executive and private investor. He serves as president of Leach Capital, LLC, San Francisco, California, as well as Foley Timber & Land Company, Perry, Florida. Mr. Leach was sworn in as the United States ambassador to France on July 16, 2001. He completed his service in France on April 15, 2005. He was also a member of the board of regents of the University of California from 1990 to 2001. He served as chairman of the board of regents from 1993 to 1995. Mr. Leach is a graduate of Yale University and attended Stanford Graduate School of Business. He attended school in Salinas, California, and graduated from Salinas Union High School in 1948. He served as an officer in the U.S. Air Force from 1953 through 1955. Mr. Leach has served as director of various companies, including chairman of Hunter Fan Company,

Memphis, Tennessee, and Shippers Development Company, Salinas, California. Mr. Leach is active in civic activities and serves on the boards of the American Friends of Versailles, the American University of Paris, the French-American Foundation, the French Heritage Society, and the Haas Business School at the University of California, Berkeley, and as an overseer of the Hoover Institution at Stanford University. Mr. Leach has been active in Republican politics for many years in the support of candidates and in California and national fundraising. He served as finance chairman of the Republican National Committee from 1995 to 1997. He currently serves on the Hoover Institution's Shultz-Stephenson Task Force on Energy Policy.

Edwin S. Lennox is a founding fellow of the Salk Institute and was also senior scientist at the Medical Research Council Laboratory of Molecular Biology in Cambridge, United Kingdom. After that he became director of research at Celltech, a UK biotech company focusing on genetic engineering and large-scale production of proteins with pharmaceutical properties. Most recently, he was CSO of a small pharmaceutical company, Pharmagenesis in Palo Alto. Research interests were mainly in microbiology and immunology as basic sciences but later work in biotechnology involved protein engineering and genetically modified proteins for clinical use. Graduate degree was in theoretical physics.

Galina Leytes's energy work is centered on being cofounder and vice president of Israel Strategic Alternative Energy Foundation (WWW.I-SAEF.ORG). She was cofounder and executive vice president of LJL BioSystems, Inc., a NASDAQ biotechnology tools company. Ms. Leytes held senior technical and information technology positions at Charles Schwab & Co., Stanford University, and in other high-technology companies. She is active in community and philanthropic activities, where she has successfully pioneered and chaired new initiatives, winning the prestigious Volunteer of the Year Award at San Francisco Jewish Community Federation. Ms. Leytes has served as board member of both private and public companies and as director in the nonprofit sector. Ms. Leytes holds a graduate degree in Computer Science from Kiev Institute of Engineering and has completed the Advanced Management Program at Stanford University's Graduate Business School.

Lev J. Leytes's energy work is centered on being cofounder and president of Israel Strategic Alternative Energy Foundation (WWW.I-SAEF.ORG). He was cofounder, chairman, and CEO of LJL BioSystems, Inc., a NASDAQ biotechnology tools company. Mr. Leytes has cofounded or held senior technical positions at other high-technology companies and served as board member of both private and public companies and as director in the nonprofit sector. Mr. Leytes has published entrepreneurship- and technology-related papers in peer-reviewed journals. He has been an invited speaker, guest lecturer, and panelist at investment, entrepreneurial, and technology forums. In 2009 he was interviewed by the Chinese *Entrepreneur* magazine, which was seeking to publish advice from leading Silicon Valley technology entrepreneurs. Mr. Leytes holds a graduate degree in Engineering from the Moscow Engineering Institute and has completed the Advanced Management Program at Stanford University.

Noah Long is a MAP Sustainable Energy Fellow for the California Energy Program. Mr. Long works on energy efficiency and renewable energy in the California Public Utility Commission, California Energy Commission, and California Air Resources Board and on implementing California's Global Warming Solutions Act, enforcing the emissions performance standard and renewable energy legislation. Mr. Long also works with the Natural Resources Defense Council's international team on energy policy in Latin America. He holds a JD from Stanford Law School and a MSc. in International Development and Environmental Policy from the London School of Economics.

Kate Marvel is a Center for Security and International Cooperation postdoctoral fellow working on energy security and sustainable infrastructure development. She received a PhD in theoretical physics at the University of Cambridge, where she was a Gates Scholar and a member of Trinity College. She chaired Cambridge University Student Pugwash and is a member of the executive board of International Student/Young Pugwash. Kate holds a BA in physics and astronomy from the University of California at Berkeley and has worked at Lawrence Berkeley Laboratory, California, and the African Institute for Mathematical Sciences in South Africa. She is active in outreach work and has lectured in settings as diverse as a community center in Lesotho, a physics institute in Tehran, and the Secret Garden Party Festival in the United Kingdom.

Franklin M. Orr, Jr., is the Keleen and Carlton Beal Professor in the Department of Energy Resources Engineering and director of the Precourt Institute for Energy at Stanford University. He served as dean of the School of Earth Sciences from 1994 to 2002 and as director of the Global Climate and Energy Project from 2002 to 2008. Previously, he worked at the U.S. Environmental Protection Agency, Shell Development Company, and the New Mexico Institute of Mining and Technology in Socorro. He holds a PhD from the University of Minnesota and a BS from Stanford University, both in chemical engineering. He is a member of the National Academy of Engineering and the board of directors of the Monterey Bay Aquarium Research Institute.

John Raisian is the Tad and Dianne Taube Director of the Hoover Institution and a senior fellow, with expertise in public policy formation and the role of government in society. The holder of a PhD in economics from the University of California, Los Angeles, John Raisian has been a Hoover fellow since 1986 and director of the Hoover Institution since 1989. He was a member of the economics faculties at the University of Washington and the University of

Houston. He also served as special assistant for economic policy and director of research and technical support in the U.S. Department of Labor during the first term of the Reagan Administration. He currently serves on the Hoover Institution's Shultz-Stephenson Task Force on Energy Policy.

Wilson Rickerson is executive vice president at Meister Consultants Group and is responsible for the firm's international energy and climate change practice. Mr. Rickerson had advised a broad range of state and local governments, international organizations, and corporations on sustainable-energy policy design and greenhouse-gas-mitigation strategies. Mr. Rickerson serves on the advisory committee for the Solar America Board of Codes and Standards and the editorial board of *BioCycle* magazine and is a policy fellow at the Center for Energy and Environmental Policy. He holds a master's degree in energy policy from the University of Delaware and a BA from the College of William & Mary.

William K. Reilly is founding partner of Aqua International Partners, a private equity fund invested in water and renewable energy companies, and senior advisor to TPG Capital, an international investment partnership. Reilly has served as administrator of the U.S. Environmental Protection Agency, president of the World Wildlife Fund, and president of the Conservation Foundation. Reilly is chairman of the ClimateWorks Foundation, chairman emeritus of the World Wildlife Fund, cochair of the National Commission on Energy Policy, chairman of the Nicholas Institute for Environmental Policy Solutions at Duke University, and a director of the Packard Foundation and the National Geographic Society. He serves on the boards of DuPont, ConocoPhillips, and Royal Caribbean International. He currently serves on the Hoover Institution's Shultz-Stephenson Task Force on Energy Policy.

Condoleezza Rice is a senior fellow and member of the Shultz-Stephenson Energy Task Force at the Hoover Institution and professor of political science at Stanford University. From January 2005 to 2009, she served as the 66th secretary of state of the United States. Before serving as America's chief diplomat, she served as assistant to the president for national security affairs from January 2001 to 2005. Rice joined the Stanford University faculty as a professor of political science in 1981 and served as Stanford's provost from 1993 to 1999. She was a senior fellow at the Hoover Institution from 1991 to 1993 and returned to the Hoover Institution after serving as provost until 2001. Rice has won two of the highest teaching honors: the 1984 Walter J. Gores Award for Excellence in Teaching and the 1993 School of Humanities and Sciences Dean's Award for Distinguished Teaching. She has authored and coauthored several books and has served as a member of the boards of directors for many corporate boards. She was a founding board member of the Center for a New Generation, an educational support fund for schools in East Palo Alto and East Menlo Park, California, and was vice president of the Boys and Girls Club of the Peninsula. In addition, she has served on several local and national boards of foundations and charitable organizations. She currently serves as a member of the board of trustees of the John F. Kennedy Center for the Performing Arts. In addition, she is a fellow of the American Academy of Arts and Sciences. Rice earned her bachelor's degree in political science, cum laude and Phi Beta Kappa, from the University of Denver in 1974; her master's from the University of Notre Dame in 1975; and her PhD from the Graduate School of International Studies at the University of Denver in 1981.

Geoffrey Rothwell is a senior lecturer and director of honors programs in the Department of Economics and the Public Policy Program and associate director of the Public Policy Program, Stanford University. His research has focused on the economics of the international nuclear power industry. His current work concerns (1) the future of the U.S. nuclear power industry, 2010–2030, and (2) the globalization of the nuclear fuel cycle, particularly uranium enrichment. He received his MA in jurisprudence and social policy from Boalt Law School, University of California, Berkeley, in 1984, and his PhD in economics from the University of California, Berkeley, in 1985. After completing a postdoctoral fellowship at the California Institute of Technology in 1986, Dr. Rothwell started working at Stanford.

Henry S. Rowen is a senior fellow at the Hoover Institution, is a professor of public policy and management emeritus at Stanford University's Graduate School of Business and a member of Stanford University's Asia/Pacific Research Center. He was assistant secretary of defense for international security affairs in the U.S. Department of Defense from 1989 to 1991. He was also chairman of the National Intelligence Council from 1981 to 1983. Rowen served as president of the RAND Corporation from 1967 to 1972 and was assistant director, U.S. Bureau of the Budget, from 1965 to 1966. From 2001 to 2004 he served on the Secretary of Defense Policy Advisory Board. In 2004–05, he served on the Presidential Commission on the Intelligence of the United States Regarding Weapons of Mass Destruction. Rowen is an expert on international security, economic development, and high-tech industries in the United States and Asia. His current research focuses on the rise of Asia in high technologies. His most recent work is coediting *Making It: The Rise of Asia in Information Technologies* (published by Stanford University Press, 2006). Among his articles are "Kim Jong Il Must Go," *Policy Review*, No. 121 October/November 2003, and "The Short March: China's Road to Democracy," *National Interest* (Fall 1996). Mr. Rowen earned a bachelor's degree in industrial management from the Massachusetts Institute of Technology in 1949 and a master's in economics from Oxford University in 1955. He currently serves on the Hoover Institution's Shultz-Stephenson Task Force on Energy Policy.

Lucy Shapiro, a professor in the Department of Developmental Biology at Stanford University School of Medicine, holds the Ludwig Chair in Cancer Research and is the director of the Beckman Center for Molecular and Genetic Medicine. She is a member of the boards of advisors of L'Institut Pasteur, the Ludwig Institute for Cancer Research, and Lawrence Berkeley National Labs. She founded the anti-infectives discovery company Anacor Pharmaceuticals, and she serves on the board of directors of Gen-Probe. Professor Shapiro has been the recipient of multiple honors, including election to the National Academy of Sciences. She was awarded the 2005 Selman A. Waksman Award from the National Academy of Sciences, the Canadian International 2009 Gairdner Award, the 2009 John Scott Award, and the 2010 Abbott Lifetime Achievement Award. She currently serves on the Hoover Institution's Shultz-Stephenson Task Force on Energy Policy.

Abraham Sofaer has been the George P. Shultz Distinguished Scholar and senior fellow at the Hoover Institution, Stanford University, since 1994, and professor of law by courtesy at Stanford Law School since 1996. His areas of specialization include diplomacy, international law, national security, terrorism, and water resources. He graduated from Yeshiva College in 1962 with a BA in history. He received his LLB degree from New York University School of Law in 1965, where he was editor-in-chief of the *Law Review* and a Root-Tilden Scholar. He clerked for Judge J. Skelly Wright on the U.S. Court of Appeals for the DC Circuit and then Associate Justice William J. Bremlau, Jr., of the U.S. Supreme Court. He served two years as a U.S. federal prosecutor in Manhattan (1967–69), ten years as professor of law at Columbia University, and six years as a U.S. district judge for the Southern District of New York. In 1985 he became the legal adviser of the U.S. Department of State and served under Secretary of State George Shultz and Secretary James Baker until 1990. From 1990 to 1994 he practiced law in Washington, DC, as a partner at Hughes, Hubbard and Reed. He currently serves on the Hoover Institution's Shultz-Stephenson Task Force on Energy Policy.

Thomas Stephenson joined Sequoia Capital in 1988 where he focuses on a broad array of information technology and health care companies. Mr. Stephenson is a former ambassador of the United States of America to the Portuguese Republic. He spent twenty-two years with Fidelity Investments in Boston where he helped found Fidelity Ventures. Tom has been very active in the affairs of Harvard University over the years and currently serves as a member of the board of overseers and its executive committee. He has also been a member of the executive committee of the board of overseers of the Hoover Institution at Stanford University, the board of advisors of the Stanford Institute for Economic Policy Research, the board of directors of Conservation International and the Wilson Center Council, and served as corporate fund vice chairman of the Kennedy Center. While living in Boston, he served for many years on boards and committees of the Tufts New England Medical Center. He was born and raised in Wilmington, Delaware, and attended Harvard College, where he received an AB in Economics. He received his MBA from Harvard Business School and a JD from Boston College Law School. He currently serves on the Hoover Institution's Shultz-Stephenson Task Force on Energy Policy.

John Taylor is the Bowen H. and Janice Arthur McCoy Senior Fellow at the Hoover Institution and the Mary and Robert Raymond Professor of Economics at Stanford University. Among other roles in public service, he served as a member of the President's Council of Economic Advisers from 1989 to 1991 and as undersecretary of the Treasury for international affairs from 2001 to 2005. He is currently a member of the California Governor's Council of Economic Advisers. His new book *Getting Off Track: How Government Actions and Interventions Caused, Prolonged, and Worsened the Financial Crisis* is an empirical analysis of the recent financial crisis. He also recently coedited *The Road Ahead for the Fed,* in which twelve leading experts, himself included, examine and debate proposals for financial reform and exit strategies from the financial crisis.

Before joining the Stanford faculty in 1984, Taylor held positions as a professor of economics at Princeton University and Columbia University. He received a BS in economics summa cum laude from Princeton and a PhD in economics from Stanford University in 1973. He currently serves on the Hoover Institution's Shultz-Stephenson Task Force on Energy Policy.

James Timbie has been the senior advisor to the undersecretary for arms control and international security for the Department of State since 1983. Prior to this he served as senior official of the Arms Control and Disarmament Agency from 1971 to 1983. Mr. Timbie was a Stanford physics graduate student from 1966 to 1971.